ERWIN BAUER'S DEER IN THEIR WORLD

ERWIN BAUER'S
DEER

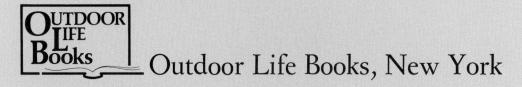 Outdoor Life Books, New York

Distributed to the trade by

Stackpole Books, Harrisburg, Pennsylvania

IN THEIR WORLD

Erwin A. Bauer

For Peggy Bauer, the best deer-stalking partner
anybody ever had

Published by

Outdoor Life Books
Grolier Book Clubs, Inc.
380 Madison Avenue
New York, NY 10017

Distributed to the trade by

Stackpole Books
Cameron and Kelker Streets
P.O. Box 1831
Harrisburg, PA 17105

Designed by George Laws at the Angelica Design Group, Ltd.; set
in 12/15 Emerson by Out of Sorts Letter Foundery; and printed by
R.R. Donnelley & Sons Company.

Library of Congress Cataloging in Publication Data

Bauer, Erwin A.
Erwin Bauer's Deer in their world.

Includes index.
1. Deer—North America.   2. Mammals—North America.
I. Title   II. Title: Deer in their world.
QL737.U55B38   1983   599.73'57   83-62704
ISBN 0-943822-23-8

Third Printing, 1987

Manufactured in the United States of America

CONTENTS

PREFACE

My first encounter with wild deer occurred in what seems to be ancient times—the hickory-smoked past. The year was 1931. I was 12 years old and I sat on a hemlock stump overlooking a balsam swamp in Schoolcraft County, Michigan. It was an early morning in October, and the sky was spitting snow onto my red wool jacket. Nervously I clutched a new longbow across my lap, with arrow nocked. Across the swamp and maybe a mile away, my mentor and oldest outdoor companion Frank Sayers had started a deer drive in my direction.

The swamp was as quiet as a tomb. I sat chilled but alert, not knowing what to expect. Suddenly two does and a fawn materialized in what a second before had been an empty scene. The phenomenon was like projecting another slide onto a vast screen.

As my heart hammered, I raised the bow and drew the arrow. But for some unfathomable reason I did not release the arrow, even though does were legal to shoot at the time. All three vanished. A split instant later I heard hoofbeats and found myself staring at what was surely the largest buck in the state, if not the world. Startled at my presence,

it broke stride in front of me and seemed to do a double take. Half in fright, I drew the bow and this time released the arrow, which ricocheted off a birch sapling, missed the buck, and went rattling away through the woods. The next sound was my own pulse pounding out of control.

I saw no more bucks that long-ago trip, nor was I ever in range again to shoot at a doe. In time I realized that the "big" buck I'd seen was really only a small forkhorn. Many other bucks I've met since then were also "the biggest ever." But that one morning—indelible in my memory—started a hopeless lifelong addiction. One way or another, I've been hunting deer ever since.

In recent decades, more and more of my hunting has been with a camera and a telephoto lens. It's not that I am opposed to deer hunting, which is an honorable pursuit and a rite of autumn across America, if not actually a necessity in many places. In fact many hardcore environmentalists and conservationists are hunters. That isn't any wonder.

But now, accompanied by my wife Peggy, I concentrate on camera hunting. We have many advantages over gun and bow hunters. First, we are never restricted by closed seasons. We can hunt the year-round—anywhere—because deer exist in every state and Canadian province. And we never have to buy a license or draw a permit to hunt our way. We can shoot a dozen or more bucks every fall without violating any law.

This whitetail has probably passed his prime years of antler growth, usually occurring at $5\frac{1}{2}$ to $6\frac{1}{2}$ years. Succeeding annual sets of antlers for this buck will decline in dimensions but will continue to show the same basic conformation.

The search for deer has taken us to some of the most exquisite and sometimes awesome corners of North America: into brooding swamps, into cool evergreen forests, and onto lonely alpine ridges and Alaskan coasts. Deer offer an exciting look into the natural scheme and are, in fact, an index of how well we are treating our environment. As a bonus, the pursuit of deer with camera, gun, or binoculars also lets us see other wildlife, other scenes, and enjoy one rich experience after another.

When we go after deer, we also get good exercise for body and spirit. Even though we have worked very hard at the game, leaving our footprints from sea level to well above timberline, it has always been rewarding and mentally relaxing. Try it and see how good it makes you feel. Many hunters claim their health is better during the deer season, which can be stretched throughout the year with camera or binoculars.

It's important to note that not all deer of the same species are carbon copies. They behave and react differently in different places. So what I say in the following pages may not hold true everywhere all the time. Some of your own observations and experiences may even contradict mine. But that only makes deer study more intriguing.

In a few words, I think it's pretty hard to match deer stalking. Anywhere.

ERWIN A. BAUER
Jackson Hole, Wyoming

The blacktail subspecies of mule deer has a black to dark-brown to reddish-brown tail that may or may not rise up when the deer is alarmed. When raised, the tail's light-colored under-hairs are not conspicuously white as the whitetail's are. Antlers on mature blacktail bucks are bifurcated, like those of the mule deer, but they tend to be smaller.

A whitetail's tail at rest is pennant-shaped and brown to reddish-brown in color with a white fringe. But when the deer is alarmed, its tail usually shoots straight up revealing a dazzling white underside and a flared white rump patch, thus giving the whitetail its name. Mature whitetail bucks have a distinctive main antler beam.

Mule deer have a sausage-shaped tail ranging from white to light-colored, the tail set in a round light-colored rump patch. Mature bucks have bifurcated antlers (two Y-shaped branches on each side). The ears are larger in relation to head size than those of whitetails, and mule deer tend to have wider faces.

 Whitetail range

 Mule deer range

Blacktail range

Here are ranges of the two native species of North American deer: the whitetail and the mule deer. Also shown is the range of the blacktail, the common name for two mule deer subspecies of relatively pure strain. Naturalists recognize many whitetail subspecies, but interbreeding has made most almost indistinguishable, except to scientists.

ERWIN BAUER'S DEER IN THEIR WORLD

Darkness fell soon after this splendid
buck in northern Ohio passed in the
sun's final shaft of light. Dawn and
dusk are the best times to search for
moving deer. This buck lived near a
heavily populated area.

CHAPTER 1
WHITETAILS

In summer, after the fawns are capable of following their mothers all the time, whitetail does and fawns tend to gather in small groups, often composed of one or more families. The bucks, meanwhile, live bachelor lives.

When our pilgrim ancestors first waded ashore more than three centuries ago, they found a nearly virgin paradise only sparsely populated by man. The land was teeming with game, without which the pilgrims might soon have perished.

Turkeys were so obliging that huge gobblers could be shot at point-blank range with blunderbuss guns. Ruffed grouse could be killed with sticks and stones. In spring and fall, waterfowl swarmed wherever wetlands existed. Shorebirds by the billions flew along the wild and beautiful coast.

The settlers also discovered another wildlife species, probably not too numerous, but otherwise remarkable. The Indians of New England ate its meat fresh or dried, and used the hide for jackets, mittens, moccasins, and leggings. Drumheads and war shields were also fashioned from the skin, and rawhide thongs formed the webbing of snowshoes and bowstrings. Implements and weapons were made from the antlers. Rattles, pipes, and other ceremonial gewgaws came from the hoofs. Shinbone marrow was used as hair oil, and bones were boiled to season maize, hominy, and beans. No part of the whitetail deer (*Odocoileus virginianus*) was wasted.

From the skimpy records that remain, we know that early settlers soon depended on deer as much as the native Indians. In fact, they hunted whitetails along the Atlantic Seaboard so relentlessly that in 1741 one Virginia settler wrote home to England:

"We so seldom see the deeres, once so many everywhere, any more." The next two centuries or so
would see whitetail numbers boom and bust for a
variety of reasons.

POPULATION DYNAMICS

Much of the eastern United States and Canada
was originally covered by vast tracts of virgin timber, where sunlight rarely penetrated to the forest
floor. Whitetail deer thrived only on forest edges
and in scattered openings. But with westward
expansion and settlement, more and more of the
original forest was cleared. The axe and plow, plus
fire, created ideal deer range from Boston and
Philadelphia all the way to the Mississippi River.
The population of eastern whitetails exploded in
the wake of the lumbermen and farmers. That was
the boom. But with passage of the Homestead Act
in 1862, a second wave of settlement swept westward. Then the deer were hunted for market
venison or simply shot to keep them out of the
crops. Herds were depleted drastically.

A few scattered records of the old market
hunting tell the story. One hunter in New York's
Catskills killed 2500 deer hunting "part-time"
before he died in 1850. Pot hunters daily brought
wagonloads of deer saddles and haunches into
downtown Chicago during the Civil War and long
after. Riverboats trading along the Ohio River could
buy venison anywhere to feed the crews and to sell
in cities such as Louisville and Cincinnati.

When deer meat eventually glutted the market,
commercial hunters continued shooting for the
fine hides. One man operating at Trader House
Creek (near present-day Waco), Texas, shipped
75,000 skins eastward between 1844 and 1853. As a
result of such killing throughout the state, Texas
established a six-buck-per-person limit per year in
1903. This was reduced to three bucks in 1907, with
the gunning season closed for five months. By the
early 1900s whitetail populations in many states had

This shows the whitetail range.

This photo was a bonus for taking
a morning walk along the edge of a
thicket, camera slung over one shoulder. Suddenly a spotted fawn simply
appeared in the sunshine. A moment
later it was gone.

Summer finds whitetail deer in reddish coats that will be shed and replaced in autumn with gray. This buck's antlers are still covered with velvet he will rub off when his antlers are full-grown.

Especially when acorns ripen and fall, southern deer are likely to be found feeding along oak hardwood ridges. This buck was photographed from a platform blind built low in a live oak.

cap of overspecialized form or function. They can succeed in a wilderness or on heavily cultivated farmland, even at the fringe of suburbia. They have the usual deer survival kit: camouflaged fawns, keen senses, generalized diet, scent glands, antlers, etc. As a wholly protected species, the whitetail is bold and obvious; where hunted it quickly becomes as formless and elusive as a wisp of woodsmoke.'' In some regions, whitetails have even overpopulated, or exceeded the carrying capacity of their range.

THE SPECIES AND SUBSPECIES

The whitetail is anywhere from 17 to 30 different deer. Or, rather, the whitetail species has that many subspecies, depending on which deer taxonomist you believe. One or another subspecies lives, or once lived, in every state except Alaska and Hawaii, and in eight provinces of Canada. The whitetail's range also extends south to Panama. Personally, I am able to distinguish the smallest, the Florida Key deer (*Odocoileus virginianus clavium*), from any of the largest, such as the prototype Virginia whitetail (*O.v. virginianus*) of the Southeast. But I cannot distinguish the subspecies beyond that, and it would be difficult for almost anyone else. In fact, some of the subspecies described long ago no longer exist. During the first half of this century, there was an effort to reestablish whitetails in areas where they had disappeared. Deer were live-trapped, transported and transshipped back and forth across the country without regard to subspecies. As a result of interbreeding, most whitetails today are simply whitetails. In general they tend to grow bigger the farther north their latitude, although nutrition is also a factor. From my observations, far-North bucks also tend to sport the heaviest, most impressive antlers.

By any name or classification, no matter where it lives, the whitetail just may be the most elegant, most graceful creature on the face of the earth. Many sportsmen regard it as the greatest game

been so decimated that hunting seasons were completely closed.

The closures, fortunately, came in time. Enough whitetail habitat still existed for a dramatic comeback, and the adaptable and prolific animal responded. Today an estimated 12 to 15 million whitetails roam the land, easily making them the most abundant and widespread of all North American big game.

Biologist-author John Madson describes it very well: ''The whitetail's dominant survival trait is psychological, for of all our deer, it is the most adaptive to changes in environment and even in human attitude. Whitetails have no apparent handi-

animal, bar none. They contend that given unlimited time, unlimited funds, and the ability to
hunt anywhere with any guide, a genuine trophy or
record-book whitetail buck would be harder to

This portrait is of a 5½- to 6½-year-old
buck, near his prime, taken near Chip-
pewa Flowage, Wisconsin.

The Columbian whitetail, now a rare
subspecies, survives (and is doing well)
in a single sanctuary near the mouth of
the Columbia River, Washington.
Separated by a great distance from
other whitetails, the Columbian subspecies probably never was abundant.

This buck sports the characteristic main beam of each antler with tines growing upward from each. The great mass and dimensions of these antlers are anything but characteristic, however.

Albinism occurs occasionally in white-tail deer herds, most often (but not always) in enclosures or refuges where the deer are not pursued by hunters or predators. I took the photo of this doe in 1971 in the Montezuma National Wildlife Refuge in New York. Albinos were common there then.

Melanism, a dark or almost black phase, is much less common than albinism among whitetails. This dark deer, photographed with a normal whitetail in central Texas in 1979, is the only one I have ever seen.

collect today than a trophy bighorn sheep, brown bear, lion, kudu, or anything else. The point is well taken.

EVOLUTION

Today's whitetail is a product of the stresses and strains of 15 million years of evolution. Scientists say it came to North America about that long ago, traveling across an isthmus between Siberia and Alaska during the Miocene Period. Somehow the whitetails survived the droughts and glaciers that almost entirely covered our country and eliminated less adaptable species such as mastodons and saber-toothed tigers. But our whitetail emerged from these incredible climatic changes, as well as the market hunting of more recent times, as the durable and beautiful animal it is.

This eastern whitetail buck is lip-curling, to help test the air for scent of a doe in estrus. This is the characteristic grimace of many big game animals throughout the rut. Whitetails are probably too numerous for their own good in several eastern states today. In these cases, heavier hunting harvests benefit the herd.

It is the beginning of the rut in west-central Manitoba. Displaying typical behavior, this buck is rubbing antlers on a tree trunk and lip-curling. The buck seemed very nervous, and he never stopped walking or searching so long as I watched.

BIRTH AND SURVIVAL

I hesitate to describe the whitetail as tough because many people assume it is gentle and frail. At first encounter, the Bambi image does seem more appropriate. But tough is really an understatement for the whitetail deer. In actuality, the animal is able to endure incredibly harsh conditions. This toughening process begins at the moment of conception during the annual rut, usually under a cold full moon, probably with a hoar frost covering the ground.

Ojibways and Crees of the North correctly called the long winter the Hunger Moon, when many creatures either hibernate or migrate to escape the cold. But a doe deer carries the fetus all winter,

without migrating or hibernating, probably on starvation rations, often in intense cold and deep snow. In addition, natural predators are most active during this time. To survive, a doe must be exceedingly tough and tenacious. The fawn she drops in May or June after a gestation of from 206 to 218 days will likely prove to be just as tough.

According to studies recently made by Norb Giessman in Missouri, a fawn is more apt to die during its first few weeks of life than a trophy buck is during hunting season. Of 52 fawns monitored in both 1980 and 1981, more than half died before the hunting season opened in mid-autumn. Similar studies in Iowa, Illinois, and Minnesota showed an equally high mortality rate. Reasons for the deaths include starvation, predation (dogs and coyotes are equally responsible), being trapped in fences, being hit by motorists, and being overrun by mowers.

Most does give birth to single fawns, although twins are not uncommon in good habitat. On two occasions, both in northern Ohio in the 1950s, I saw triplets. In 1853 the naturalist Audubon reported a Carolina doe with four fawns. And in April 1949, a large doe killed by a car near Chautauqua, New

Spotted fawns with large brown eyes are deceptively frail in appearance, and are vulnerable to predation until they are about a month old. But if they make it past that difficult period, they will be able to run as fast as adults and to withstand the cold northern winters as well.

York, was autopsied and found to be carrying four fully developed fawns. This was only the third recorded instance of such fecundity in whitetails.

Few have ever seen a fawn's birth, which is usually quick and appears to be painless. Instinctively, the mother promptly eats the placental sac and licks up any waste fluids that might attract predators—another survival tactic. But more interesting is the fact that during birth and for a period thereafter, the hair on a doe's metatarsal glands stands erect and emits an odor. If a predator approaches, the doe consequently can flee and attract the predator to herself and away from the relatively odorless fawn. Still, it is estimated that one in 10 or 11 fawns perish during the first week of life. The odds improve after that.

Newborn, with 250 to 350 cream-colored spots, fawns remain almost motionless and isolated for a few days after birth. I have nearly walked on the well-camouflaged youngsters before seeing them. Mothers desert fawns during most of the day, returning at intervals and at night to nurse them with milk that has about three times as much protein and butterfat as the most nutritious cow's milk. The weaning process goes on for three or four months, sometimes lasting almost to the rut in November or December.

A typical whitetail fawn is self-sufficient by the time the first maple leaves begin to fall in autumn. I have seen more than one jump cleanly over a six-foot barrier from a standing position. A six-month fawn can sprint 30 m.p.h. over a woodland obstacle course, keeping pace with older animals. If the young survives its first fall hunting season, it must pass the same cold and starvation test its mother passed the winter before.

REPRODUCTION

Dr. Rob Wegner, writing in the monthly *Deer & Deer Hunting* magazine, says that the fawn sex ratio is about one to one, with slightly more males

Whitetails are wary from an early age. This fawn has just heard the shutter of Peggy's camera to the left. I shot the instant the fawn looked up.

Luck is also important when deer watching. Sitting in a blind in late afternoon with the sun over my shoulder, I watched intently in another direction. But a soft sound behind caused me to turn around—and there stood this doe, watching me, backlit against a mesquite tree. This experience serves to point up the value of watching in all directions all the time.

dropped. There is growing evidence that well-fed does produce more females, while undernourished does produce more males. Biologists have no idea why this is true. But within a week of fawning time, there are more females than males left alive, and that ratio continues to widen as the animals grow older. Female fawns also remain with their mothers much longer, for up to two years after birth.

I should insert a few figures here about a white-tail doe's astounding productivity. During a 15-year period, one tame New York female dropped 23

When wolves are introduced to deer
territory, wolf and deer populations
soon strike a healthy balance.

fawns, including twins at the age of 17. We must
keep in mind that a doe in the wild is unlikely to live
half that long, of course. A Wisconsin doe that died
at age 19 produced twins through her 18th spring.
In theory only, a healthy whitetail buck and doe
pair could become a herd of 22 deer in five years. Or
make that 189 deer in 10 years! Such projections
are only theoretical, and indicate the potential population growth in a perfect, predator-free environment.

Few of the world's wild animals are equipped
with as many efficient escape mechanisms as the
whitetail. Any whitetail is a lithe, powerful jumper.
From a running start, seemingly effortless bounds
of 25 to 30 feet are not unusual. I once measured the
leap of a dog-frightened doe at 27 feet. In that leap
she'd cleared a deadfall that measured three feet

No animal is more graceful when
bounding at high speed through a
forest than the whitetail, which is also
agile and can disappear like a ghost.

I've seen far more white flags waving and disappearing than I would have preferred. Although most whitetails raise the tail immediately at the first sign of danger, this one didn't, though his white rump patch is flared in alarm. Bucks will often sneak off unseen, rather than flush.

This Ohio whitetail doe had been browsing on the near edge of this stream. I figured she would flush across the stream because that's where the nearest escape cover was. So I focused on the center of the stream and came up with this shot.

high. No other American hoofed animal can vanish from sight so swiftly and so gracefully. By contrast, the whitetail's closest cousin, the mule deer, bounces away somewhat stiff-legged, although this gait is faster than it looks.

When escaping under stress, a whitetail buck in winter becomes a horizontal blur. Far too often a deer's great bounds have merged into a gallop too fleet for my camera shutter to freeze. But no matter how swiftly a deer is traveling, it can stop abruptly and turn in a totally different direction, a maneuver you might expect to splinter its thin front legs. But the whitetail has a ball-bearing anatomy that makes this and other acrobatics easy. A whitetail's forelegs do not connect directly to the skeleton, but are separated by a neoprene-tough cartilage that acts as a heavy-duty shock absorber.

Some wild animals survive as escape artists, being swift afoot, or at least swifter than their predators. Others live by camouflage or subterfuge, or they rely on their keen senses alone. But whitetails exploit all of these defenses. Their color and normal movements blend into bleak, bare North American woodlands after leaves have fallen. I have often seen deer almost evaporate into their environments.

A whitetail has splendid hearing, a phenomenal sense of smell, and good eyesight, even in semi-darkness. (There is some evidence that deer are not totally color-blind, as was long thought.) On numerous occasions, when wandering through a dense woods at sunset, I have flushed deer and heard them bound away, without colliding with any obstacle—neatly, as if in broad daylight.

Vision is difficult to measure or evaluate in any animal. But I have heard deer hunters and other observers state flatly that a whitetail's vision is the equivalent of a sharp eight-power telephoto lens. Exaggerated claim or not, one fact is true: A healthy deer can spot an unnatural movement from a great distance. Actually, it is movement as much as anything else that alerts a deer to the presence of danger.

Still, the ears have it. Studies have revealed that a deer's hearing is so acute it can distinguish the footfall of a bear, or another deer, from a human tread without even bothering to look up. The sound is transmitted instantly to the brain, and if the sound is human, the deer is immediately ready to bolt. From long observation, I know that a whitetail hearing human sounds may not show visible alarm, even though it is aware and ready to flee.

Here is something else to consider. By constantly "focusing" or "tuning" its ears in every direction, a whitetail always knows what is happening all around. That way it keeps track of other deer in the herd. Without actually seeing them, it knows

Even as it feeds, the whitetail buck is alert and watchful. That eye is suddenly focused on me, camouflaged and sitting in a nearby tree. A split-second later and the buck was gone.

what they are doing and where. Francis Sell, a veteran Oregon writer and deer watcher, noted that a deer can hear another deer walking in heavy cover up to 65 yards away. The sound of this movement is either reassuring or alarming, depending on the pace. A slow speed is usually reassuring, while a fast pace can be cause for alarm. Sell also believes that the careful, stylized, mincing step of a whitetail has two purposes. First, it makes deer move-

This photo illustrates how difficult it is to spot a motionless deer, even if it is standing out in the open, even with a speckling of snow on the vegetation. A person whose eyes are not attuned to the outdoors might never have seen this buck.

ments less alarming to other deer; second, it does not cancel out other normal woodland sounds.

Once, when sitting in a blind in Kent County, Maryland, I conducted my own test of deer hearing. Within my view were nine deer feeding in an open field on the edge of a woodlot. The nearest were about 20 yards away, the farthest about 80 yards. A slight crosswind was blowing. At intervals I worked the zipper on my jacket up and down and scraped a fingernail and a blackberry thorn on my jacket. I also scuffed the plywood floor of the blind with the lugged soles of my boots. I shot several exposures of film with my 35mm camera using the motor drive (automatic film advance) on half the frames, and the other half without the motor drive.

The closest deer looked up instantly at *all* of these sounds, as did some of the deer at mid-distance. This action, this looking up, also alerted all the farthest deer that may or may not have heard my sounds. Although I am convinced that none of the deer actually spotted me, my noises made them nervous enough to make them gradually drift away into heavy cover and out of sight.

FOODS

What do whitetails eat? The answer is that they eat a greater variety of plants and parts of plants than we could list in this book. In one sense whitetails might be described as picky eaters. When given a choice they prefer to eat browse (leaves, twigs, young shoots of woody plants and vines) and forbs (so-called weeds and other flowering plants and vines). In some regions deer eat some grass, but only when it is green and succulent. Nationwide, the most severe deer food shortages usually occur in winter and, to a lesser degree, in late summer. Adequate forage is normally available during spring and fall. A large variety of foods in a given area makes for the best whitetail habitat.

Tennessee biologist Dick Hurd divides deer foods into three categories: "ice cream, meat and potatoes, and spinach foods." In areas with light deer populations, the animals can concentrate on the preferred, or "ice-cream," foods. As numbers increase, they must depend more and more on less desirable foods. Surveys of the amount and kinds of browse eaten always reveal whether the deer population is in balance with its food supply or not. When research shows that deer are eating spinach food, it is a warning of deteriorating habitat. New York biologists have estimated that a whitetail in winter needs six pounds of browse per day to survive until April or May. Once, as a test, I picked that much winter deer forage by hand and discovered I needed many hours for the job. The six pounds bulked to $16\frac{1}{2}$ quarts of cedar, maple, wild apple, and red oak tips.

Just as some humans have curious appetites, so do some whitetails. At least one doe in Michigan was observed actually eating fish. Far more common is for deer to wade flank-deep into sluggish streams to eat algae. In 1955 biologist Gene Knoder was hunting in the tangled hill country of southeastern Ohio near an illegal whiskey still when he shot a

In early autumn it isn't unusual to find several small whitetail bucks in a group, as here in the Wyoming Black Hills. However, the bucks do not remain inactive long. Instead, the young males constantly spar and test one another.

By rattling some antlers together, I coaxed this buck fairly close to a blind where I sat with a camera on a tripod. But some movement or odor suddenly spooked the animal. I snapped the shutter just as he turned and ran away.

fine, fat 11-point buck. When he field-dressed the animal, he found that its stomach contained sour mash. That strange diet may have accounted for the downfall of what became known as the Moonshine Buck.

WEIGHT AND SIZE

There is an immense amount of variation in deer size. Mature male Coues whitetails of the Southwest rarely exceed 100 pounds. Murry Burnham and I weighed a Carmen Mountains whitetail buck of the Texas Rio Grande country, estimated to be $6\frac{1}{2}$ to $7\frac{1}{2}$ years old, nearly the maximum age, at 105 pounds. At the other extreme, a hog-dressed (entrails removed) Nebraska buck was weighed at 310 pounds. It would have weighed 380 pounds on the hoof. New York Conservation Department officers once weighed a Mud Lake buck at 388 pounds. Perhaps some of the occasional reports of 400-pounds-plus whitetail bucks taken in Saskatchewan and Manitoba are true, but I know of none that are official.

The heaviest buck I have ever seen was an Ohio animal that tipped the scales at 214 pounds, dressed. To tell the truth, a 200-pounder is a very big deer. For example, the average weight of Pennsylvania bucks is about 115 pounds. In Maine and New York it is less than 150. Body weight is not necessarily an index of antler size, a subject I cover in Chapter 5, but large deer usually have large antlers. On the average, North American whitetail does are from two-thirds to three-fourths the size of males of the same age living in the same environment.

The first light of morning usually establishes the best time for deer photography, especially so for the very shy Carmen whitetail. This was filmed in the Chisos Mountains, Texas.

Carmen Mountains deer, a small white-tail subspecies, live in the scrub oak forests just below Casagrande in Texas Big Bend country and in similar habitat over the Rio Grande River into Mexico. Although numerous, these deer are not always easy to find.

A motionless deer even in sparse cover is not always easy to see because it blends into its surroundings so well, as here in south Texas. Whenever searching or watching for deer, travel slowly and deliberately, pausing often to study the habitat all around.

This buck had a splendid rack and provided one of my favorite whitetail photographs. Standing in the glow of an autumn morning, the buck is as fat as bucks ever get, sleek, and alert. His neck is swollen from the rut. Soon after my camera shutter clicked here, the buck turned around and drove two other bucks from his territory.

INTELLIGENCE

It is impossible to watch, hunt, or photograph whitetail deer and not wonder about their intelligence. Too many of them have slipped away from me too easily for me not to wonder. I have been outwitted so often that I am now philosophical about it. Of course it's true that deer can become almost tame and confiding in areas where they are never hunted and where natural predators are no threat to them. Such deer soon learn to freeload on grain and other enticements in gardens and backyards. But almost everywhere else, the word *furtive* describes whitetail very well.

Whitetails exist almost anonymously in many places, especially in the eastern United States where their nearest human neighbors often don't know they're even there until deer are killed on the highways. This happens mainly during the "Crazy Moon"—the annual rut—when a lot of the deer's natural caution temporarily evaporates. This is doubly true regarding the older, larger males. I have known deer-hunting seasons in Ohio and elsewhere in the Midwest to pass in certain communities without a single trophy buck being seen or taken. But then the annual winter roadkill invariably includes a number of massive males, some big enough to be reported to the newspapers. Because of the rut, the same deer that elude humans in their own environment, suddenly cannot do so when the humans are in their cars.

This aspen grove is typical cover in Manitoba's Riding Mountains, where many whitetails are likely to be found in autumn. This area is near the northern limits of the whitetail's range.

WILINESS

The whitetail's wiliness is well-established by scientific experiment. In a well-publicized study some years ago, Michigan wildlife officials stocked 39 whitetail deer in the one-square-mile, escape-proof enclosure of the Cusino Wildlife Experiment Station. The mixed hardwood, pine, and swampland inside the enclosure was typical of the state's deer habitat. Nine of the 39 deer inside were bucks. During favorable weather and with a tracking snow covering the ground, six experienced hunters were permitted to hunt within the area. Before the hunt, one local newspaper columnist sneered that it wasn't a very sporting proposition.

He was correct. It wasn't sporting—for the hunters, that is. Four days elapsed before any of them even saw a buck. And 51 total hours of hunting were required to kill one buck, confined, mind you, where it couldn't escape. It was a remarkable testimony to a remarkable creature's wiliness.

In another experiment in South Dakota, a whitetail buck was fitted with a radio-transmitter collar and blaze-orange plastic ear streamers before being released into an open hunting area just ahead of the hunting season. Via transmitter the biologists could monitor the deer's movements and behavior no matter where it went or what it did. As it turned out, a whole week passed and not one hunter even saw the animal, although some were known to have passed within 40 yards of those orange streamers.

During the second week a hunter practically stepped on the buck where it was hiding, orange streamers and all, no doubt watching the man from its bed in a thicket. But the encounter was so sudden and the hunter so startled that the deer was able to escape unhurt. No hunter ever did bag that wily buck , which eventually shed the streamers and the radio collar.

CHAPTER 2
MULE DEER

It was September in Wyoming's Gros Ventre Mountains. Gap Puche and I wolfed down an early breakfast, saddled two horses, and left his base camp at about 9000 feet, in total darkness. For about three hours we rode steadily upward, pausing now and then to rest the horses. The animals plodded easily along the thin trail—which I couldn't even see in the predawn blackness—as if traveling in broad daylight. But I knew that in places we were riding along the edge of eternity, and maybe it was better *not* to see. The trail switchbacked along the face of a sheer cliff that fell away 1000 feet to Crystal Creek tumbling below.

Just before sunrise we reached a pass and rode across an alpine meadow glittering with frost.

This is typical summer range of mule deer in western Wyoming. Does browse the basins and high meadows, while bucks live in loftier, more remote sites that are often above timberline. Mule deer share summer range with elk, bears, and even bighorn sheep.

Pursuing deer inevitably takes you to some of the most magnificent scenes in America, especially in winter. This photo was made on a lonely ridge after a Thanksgiving Day snowfall.

There we stopped to watch some indistinct dark forms—a herd of elk—slip away into dark timber. When the meadow narrowed to nothing, we rode up a final steep pitch and emerged onto a bare and windswept landscape. We might have been on another planet, but were really well above timberline. Riding a half mile farther, now bathed by the first bronze sunlight, we dismounted near a ledge where we could crouch to study the wilderness all around. Scattered snowbanks still survived from last winter. I shivered in the bitter wind, and tried to retreat deeper into my heavy jacket.

There was method rather than some madness in coming to this place at this time. Gap is a busy, successful outfitter who each September takes big-game hunters into the Gros Ventre country after elk and bighorn sheep. Now it was a few days before the opening of sheep season and Gap was scouting to learn where the rams were. I rode along eagerly because I can never pass up an opportunity to roam through wilderness country, especially in September. Autumn in the northern Rockies just may be the nearest thing on earth to Paradise Found.

Through field glasses, the two of us scanned every corner of that lonely, high-mountain real estate for a glimpse of bighorn rams. Nothing. Apparently the sheep had deserted this area for greener pasture, and Gap would have to search areas farther away. We were somewhat disappointed, and I idly kicked a loose rock with my foot. The rock rolled down a steep bare slope and seemed to explode only 200 feet below us. Spooked from its bed by the falling rock, a mule deer buck was suddenly on its feet and running toward a deep draw to our right.

Taken by surprise, I watched the animal race across terrain that might have deterred a sheep or any other heavy-hoofed animal. Finally, far away,

Peggy and I met this buck on a ski trail near Banff in Alberta. Farther along the same trail, we saw many other deer in what seemed to be a popular bedding area.

This shows the mule deer range.

the mule deer stopped to look back at us—in hunting season, a sometimes fatal characteristic of the species—and I focused the glasses on it. I believe that muley buck was the second largest muley I have ever seen alive. And I have always wondered what it was doing where only bighorn sheep or eagles ought to be.

WHERE BIG BUCKS GO

Since that morning I have learned a lot more about mule deer. For one thing, I now live in the heart of mule deer country and see them almost every day, occasionally right from the back porch. Peggy and I have also devoted whole summers to backpacking high in the Wyoming Tetons, in Montana's Beartooths and the Bob Marshall Wilderness, in Idaho's Sawtooths, in spectacular Zion National Park, Utah, in the Guadalupe Mountains of west Texas, and in Jasper National Park, Alberta. Although it is possible to encounter mule deer anywhere in these places, almost invariably we have found the biggest bucks, those with the most

massive antlers and heaviest bodies, in the highest elevations, often where it seems a deer would never venture. More than anything else, the North American mule deer (*Odocoileus hemionus*) dwells in some of the most beautiful and unspoiled parts of the continent. Of all our deer, muleys most symbolize to me our too rapidly vanishing wild places.

Mule deer in Utah often spend at least part of the winter in canyons such as this. In fact, a herd of deer fled this scene when I paused to shoot this photo.

POPULATION DYNAMICS

Scientifically, we do not know as much about mule deer as we do about whitetails. More people are interested in, and hunt for, whitetails, so more money and greater efforts have been spent researching them. Historically, mule deer have never been hunted as heavily as whitetails, nor do they tend to live in heavily populated parts. But we do know that the mule deer population is undergoing a slow decline, a fact that became evident about 1970. The winning of the West, or losing of it, depending on your viewpoint, has been taking a terrible toll on mule deer and other wildlife. The deer simply cannot prosper where people insist on building condominium communities in critical winter habitat, or building roads and drilling gas wells in a pristine wilderness area. It is the type of senseless, mindless "progress" that we will someday regret.

The high country of northern New Mexico, half evergreen, half quaking aspen, punctuated with open meadows, supports a healthy herd of deer. Elk and black bears also live in here.

The grass and sagebrush foothills here in southwestern Montana are an important wintering area for mule deer that summer in the higher ranges in the distance. The annual rut takes place in this scene.

Especially in arid areas, mule deer are able to go for long periods without drinking. I have not seen mule deer drink often. But here in the Alberta Rockies, a handsome buck pauses for several minutes to refuel before crossing a cold stream.

The early naturalist, Ernest Thompson Seton, estimated the North American mule deer population to be about 10 million when the mountain-men, beaver trappers, and trailblazers followed in the footsteps of Lewis and Clark in the early 1800s. This estimate may be a little on the high side. Of course, the western Indians always hunted deer, but probably made no dent in the population because bison were bigger, more useful, and much easier to kill. Still, Seton believed that by about 1905 the mule deer population had dropped by about 95 percent, or to a 500,000 head count nationwide. A strange combination of overexploitation and preservation caused the decline, the exploitation occurring in the form of unrestricted commercial hunting in some places, the "preservation" occurring in areas where deer were protected completely, such as in the classic example of Arizona's Kaibab herd. I cover the Kaibab herd in Chapter 8.

Market hunting was always the heaviest where transcontinental railroads were being built, and around gold, logging, and mining settlements. The deer were wiped out within vast areas surrounding every gold camp from Sutter's Mill to Placerville in California. The same was true from Leadville to Silverton, Colorado, a century ago, and history just may be repeating itself around the oil and gas boom areas of Utah and Wyoming today.

In past years, people used to blame forest fires for wildlife declines. But in actuality the prevention of forest fires, which has gone on in the West for several decades now, has caused an immense change in mule deer habitat. Mule deer had always thrived on the regeneration of forest and forage plants that grew lush in the aftermaths of fires, avalanches, and even of certain kinds of cutting or timber harvest. But without fires or the equivalent, climax forest floors are relatively barren places where few deer can live.

THE SPECIES

In many respects mule deer are not all that different from whitetails. Biologist Harry Harju of the Wyoming Game and Fish Department believes that constantly increasing hunting pressure causes mule deer to become more like whitetails every year —in other words, more wary and more furtive. Despite this, muleys are purely western rather than eastern. Both species do use the same range in a few scattered areas such as South Dakota's Black Hills, Montana's Flathead Valley, and Texas's Big Bend country along the Rio Grande River. Yet even when they share habitat, they simply do not interbreed as some people insist.

On average, mule deer are also heavier and stockier of build than whitetails, with the males having heavier, more-massive antlers. Searching through much of the available data, I figure that the average weight of a western mule deer buck is about 175 pounds, with some northern animals averaging to 200 pounds and some deer of the dry Southwest averaging 150 pounds. If you rub elbows long enough with mule deer hunters, you are certain to hear reports of 400- to 500-pound specimens. But the odds against such a giant are staggering. The largest know mule deer probably was a buck which, according to biologist Dr. Ian McTaggert Cowan, weighed 475 pounds. Cowan did not say where or when this animal was weighed, but it may have been in his home province of British Columbia.

The two small bucks with uneven antlers may have been twin fawns two years before. I shot this picture near Mesa Verde, Colorado, where muley bucks tend to have impressive racks.

Distinguishing itself from the white-tail, this mule deer buck shows typical bifurcated antlers (two Ys on each side) and a black-tipped tail set in a white rump patch.

In the field, a number of distinctive marks differentiate a mule deer from a whitetail. The ears, which give the mule deer its name, are considerably bigger. Muleys have white on their faces with contrasting, usually very dark, and sometimes solid black foreheads. Whitetails have larger, broader, leaf-shaped tails that are white underneath. But the most noticeable, quickly spotted mark of the mule deer is its white rump and thin, black-tipped tail. If all this sounds like fine distinctions, studying the photographs in this book will help you tell the two American deer species apart.

HOW TO SPOT MULE DEER

A motionless mule deer, particularly one that is bedded in gray-green sagebrush or in the shadows, is a difficult creature to see. But I have learned to spot them because of their four-chambered stomachs. Let me explain.

One morning in Montana, Peggy and I had been photographing a small mule deer buck in heavy cover along the Jocko River. Throughout the session the animal kept looking back toward one spot, as if it were being followed or accompanied. We couldn't see anything until I finally noticed a small, slight, regular up-and-down movement deep in the dry brown brush. Focusing on that spot through my 600mm telephoto lens, I could barely make out the outline of a buck that was much larger than the first one. It was bedded, facing directly toward us. The telltale motion I noticed was the lower jaw chewing cud. Like all deer, livestock,

Peggy and I spotted this bedded buck from a long distance after studying the area through 10× binoculars. At first the motionless deer seemed to be just a stump. It did not move until we made noise setting up a tripod.

antelope, and giraffes, mule deer are ruminants (with four stomach compartments) that seldom stop chewing when at rest. Such very slight motion may catch your eye too, if you are looking for it.

FAWNS

Hiking in mule deer country can be a rich experience at any time of the year, and springtime has its own special rewards. First, the greatest wild-flower show on earth is just beginning. Soon after the snows melt, entire mountainsides become as brilliant and multicolored as an oriental tapestry with blooms such as buttercup and columbine, paintbrush and beargrass. One morning, bending to photograph a clump of yellow balsamroot, Peggy noticed something out of place just behind it. There, with thin legs tucked under its cream-spotted, earth-colored coat, ears laid back, barely breathing, was a fawn, trying not to blink an eye to

The bedded deer is easy enough to see in this semi-closeup. When viewed from a distance, however, it blends into its background surprisingly well. Only the almost imperceptible motion of the lower jaw, chewing, betrayed the deer's position to me. It did not linger long after hearing the sound of the motor drive on my camera.

Notice the buck just barely visible in the bottom of the picture. This is a typical place for such a buck to bed during daylight. While remaining inconspicuous at this vantage point, it can watch a vast area.

betray its presence. No doe mother or any other deer was in sight. The fawn appeared barely alive, and at first glance seemed to be abandoned by its mother. But we knew better and hurried away as quickly as possible.

The fawn was merely exhibiting the instinctive survival behavior that has served mule deer ever since the species evolved. Ken Hamlin and Shawn Riley, biologists with Montana's deer research program, have found many fawns in similar situations, but they have gone several steps farther. By radio-collaring some mule deer fawns, they have been able to track them during the first year of life.

One interesting conclusion is that mule deer does visit their fawns very infrequently during the first few weeks. And that enforced solitude probably helps keep predators away when the fawns are most vulnerable. According to Riley, "Does visit fawns two or three times daily, primarily to nurse them, usually during the first hour or two of daylight, in late evening, and maybe once during midafternoon. There is no definitive visitation pattern, though.

"The doe picks the general area for the fawn to bed, but the fawn selects its own site. Twin fawns are bedded an average of 75 yards apart during the first few weeks, but this distance decreases throughout the summer. The mothers go off feeding on their own, leisurely when browse is abundant, up to one and one half miles away from the bedded young. But normally the does stay within 300 yards and within sight of their young."

The fawn that Peggy and I found hidden behind the balsamroot was safer than it may have appeared. Motionless, it probably wouldn't catch a coyote's eye unless the coyote happened to come almost as close as we did. Licked clean by the mother, the fawn gives off little or no scent. And the mottled coat is an effective camouflage kit.

Shawn Riley has often seen coyotes pass within 20 yards of fawns in their freeze-survival beha-

vior without spotting them. But a restless fawn that moves to a cooler place in the shade is unduly exposing itself. According to Riley, "I'm convinced most fawn mortality occurs when they are up (traveling) with the doe, and Ken Hamlin has seen a coyote spot and catch a fawn at this time."

When ready to feed her fawn, a doe returning to the bedding area typically begins making low bleating noises or grunts when she is about 100 yards away. That is an invitation for the fawn to get up and join its mother. Bucks have nothing to do with raising fawns, preferring instead to stay far away in high, cool places, living bachelor lives. Paintings that show a deer "family" intact— doe, buck, and fawn together—are totally unrealistic.

There is a lesson in all this. The biggest danger to newborn fawns, whitetails as well as mule deer, is from well-meaning people. If you ever find a fawn, go away and leave it alone. Its mother is no doubt nearby and watching you. Abandonment of fawns by healthy does is virtually unheard of.

This Wyoming mule deer buck is following the trail of a doe in the peak of estrus. Throughout a doe's estrus, which may last 30 hours, the buck is never more than a few feet distant unless driven farther by a stronger male. The actual mating, which people seldom see, usually takes place at night.

MIGRATION PATTERNS AND THE RUT

With some exceptions mule deer tend to spend summers in high, cool places, with the bucks inhabiting the highest retreats of all. After the fawns grow strong and agile enough to follow their mothers all day long, mule deer begin to gather in larger and larger herds, moving about to take advantage of the best forage. When hiking or riding in the mountains, we have frequently come onto mountainsides that were almost alive with mule deer. On the next mountain there may be none. A day or two later, the herd may change mountains.

In the northern Rockies, two changes occur as late autumn blends into winter. First, the deer gradually drift downward to lower elevations, staying ahead of the descending snowline, with does and fawns ahead of the bucks. It is the deep snow that drives them, not the increasingly cold weather. Although I have seen deer traveling downward at all times of day, most of this movement occurs at night. Second, the annual rut begins when the mature bucks finally join the does. All summer long the low slopes near our Wyoming home, at about 6500 feet elevation, are virtually barren of deer.

All senses of the mule deer—sight, scent, and hearing—are keen. To reach maturity a buck must depend heavily on all three. But many hunting guides believe that the mule deer's nose is its best defense.

This mule deer buck of the Alberta Rockies was fighting and slashing at the tree with its antlers when I appeared on the scene. I could hear the clatter against bare limbs from far away, and followed the sound. The buck stopped performing when it saw me and quickly walked away.

Suddenly, toward the end of November and usually lasting until mid-December, we can watch the mating activities not far away.

The rut is an especially frantic, busy time for the bucks, which seem to eat and sleep very little then. There is constant chasing, dueling, maneuvering, and restless moving about in search of does in estrus. Many times we have watched bucks in head-to-head combat. Most rutting fights are quick, sharp clashes in which there is a clear-cut winner, but in which the loser is seldom driven too far away from the action. I have seen only one buck badly injured from such a skirmish. One of his eyes had been pierced by an antler point. Otherwise he appeared healthy.

It is the fortunate person who comes upon a doe in estrus, a period which lasts only about 30 hours, because all the deer "action" in the vicinity will be centered right where that doe is. All the bucks of breeding age will be on hand, attracted like steel filings to a magnet. This is when the most dominant, red-eyed buck will be hard-pressed to drive others away from the female. During this period bucks show tremendous stamina and determination.

Peggy and I once camped for several nights in an area that has long been a mule deer rutting place in early December. Although we could not see what was taking place, we listened from our sleeping bags all night to the endless rushing and charging about outside the tent. Several times I was awakened by the crack of antlers. In the morning there were fresh hoofprints all around our dead campfire. Through the tent flaps I could see a doe bedded down about 75 yards away, and four bucks were standing in a rough circle nearby, eyeing one another suspiciously. Because the rut leaves male mule deer weak and exhausted, they are often easier prey for predators than does are as winter, the critical time for survival, approaches.

The evening before this photo was taken in Wyoming, Peggy and I watched this buck drive two others out of the vicinity. Two does are hidden in the shadows of the background. The area immediately surrounding this place is very busy during the rut.

Two mule deer bucks of equal size go head-to-head in a rutting season duel, while another good buck watches. This is a serious contest because a doe in estrus, the prize to the winner, is standing just outside the photograph.

The sparring in this photo is not too serious. These muley bucks are young and are simply sparring to test one another—training for the future. The actual fighting and ultimate breeding are monopolized by bigger, more mature bucks.

Severe winters with deep snowfall take a heavy toll on mule deer that are forced to concentrate in a few lowland areas, often close to towns. Besides the scarcity of survival food, the already-weakened deer are vulnerable to free-roaming dogs. The roadkill is also heavy at this time.

The Wyoming winter is one that mig illustrate a Christmas card. But mule deer have a difficult time during a severe winter. They have been at-tracted to this area along the Hoback River by handouts of hay placed by well-meaning citizens of Jackson Hole Biologists question the value of such winter feeding.

Mule deer can survive most winters fairly well if enough food is available and if they are not harassed by humans or dogs. Often they simply wait out storms, sitting motionless for long periods as falling flakes collect but do not melt on their insulated coats.

WINTER

Winter can be a terrible season for mule deer, especially if there is abnormally high snowfall. A few decades ago mule deer could migrate from the mountains into certain valleys ahead of the snow, and continue to move until they found open or windswept areas where they could pass the coldest, grimmest months. But this is no longer the case. Today, almost everywhere, the traditional migration routes are blocked by cattle ranches, towns, and other developments. Few suitable wintering areas remain, and even those are vanishing. Around many western towns mule deer herds are constantly harassed by free-running dogs, and the toll of deer run down on the highways is much too high. Spring never comes too soon. Even in the best of springtimes, however, deer numbers are greatly reduced from those of the previous autumn.

CHANGING PATTERNS

The arrival of spring doesn't immediately wipe away the hazards and problems facing mule deer. As they slowly migrate back to the high country these days, they encounter more and more land that is already overgrazed by domestic livestock. I am writing now of public land—your land and mine—administered by both the U.S. Forest Service and Bureau of Land Management. In many areas the overgrazed land is a national disgrace, with consequences stretching far beyond the damage to mule deer, elk, moose, bighorn, and pronghorn habitat.

Although sporting a small set of antlers for its body, this buck nonetheless has a better than average rack for a desert mule deer in the Guadalupe Mountains of extreme west Texas. Muleys are abundant along the hiking trails in this picturesque wilderness.

From late autumn through winter, we have often found mule deer here in the bottoms along the Virgin River of Zion National Park. In summertime, the valley is alive with people, so the deer migrate into higher country where only a few hikers travel the trails.

In his splendid book *The Deer of North America*, probably the most complete and best illustrated reference on the subject, Leonard Lee Rue III correctly notes that "mule deer are not as adaptable as whitetails. Until recently the species did not have as much exposure to the encroachment of civilization." According to Rue, mule deer "are becoming warier but less spooky."

Lately it seems as if we've been seeing more and more mule deer on the high, dry plains of Wyoming's pronghorn country. Somehow they seem out of place there. And now and then we even flush a large buck from a hidden and waterless sage-

This muley buck, of a desert race, was photographed near Carlsbad, New Mexico. In this region, even full-grown males such as this one lack widespread or heavy antlers.

brush draw. One such buck remained absolutely motionless until we had passed by, but within 50 feet of it, before it bolted. That is characteristic whitetail behavior.

Another factor working against the mule deer is that the whitetail is still expanding its range westward and growing in numbers. Normally the two do not directly compete for available food, but irrigation and agricultural practices are subtly altering habitat in favor of whitetails. Inexorably, mule deer are being squeezed out.

Whitetails also carry a parasitic brain worm to which they have become almost immune. Mule deer that have lived for a long time in the same environment with whitetails have also become almost immune. But there is trouble when whitetails move into new muley areas because the local mule deer become infected when they eat the microscopic snails that are hosts to the worm. Resultant situations have been fatal to many mule deer in recent years.

Despite the problems, mule deer are thriving today in suitable habitat where they always have. They are handsome, highly attractive animals and the landscape of the American West would be far less exciting without them.

Mule deer have adapted somewhat to ranching and agriculture. This buck is one of several we found living in heavy vegetation along an irrigation ditch. Apparently it never traveled in summer to the nearby mountains.

CHAPTER 3
BLACKTAILS

Early one autumn Peggy and I spent a good bit of time exploring Washington's beautiful Olympic Peninsula, from the Hoh Rain Forest in western Olympic National Park to Hurricane Ridge high on the park's eastern side. Aside from its immense beauty, the peninsula is remarkable for its rainfall pattern. Sweeping eastward across Pacific Ocean swells, the wind picks up moisture from the warm sea. When the air reaches the coast, it rises and meets the cold Olympic Mountains barrier, where it is soon chilled and then wrung almost dry. As a result, the small area from the Hoh rain forest to Mount Olympus is the wettest place in the continental United States, with about 200 inches of precipitation every year. The area just 50 miles eastward, around Sequim, is the driest coastal region north of southern California, with an annual average rainfall of less than 17 inches.

Despite the great differences in rainfall in this region, the Columbian blacktail thrives throughout. It also thrives from dark thickets near sea level to barren outcrops more than a mile high.

Starting before daybreak one hazy morning, Peggy and I began slowly climbing up the steep lung-buster of a trail from the Heart of the Hills (Olympic Park) Road to Klahhane Ridge. The climb was extremely tough going, especially with 20 pounds of camera gear in each backpack. But the day promised to clear and our mission was to photograph the mountain goats that live in that lonely, lofty hideaway. As we hoped, we found a herd of

We backpacked our camera gear on Hurricane Ridge, Olympic National Park, in hopes of photographing mountain goats. But we forsook the goat idea when we encountered these two blacktail bucks, probably siblings, wearing their reddish summer coats.

goats near the crest of the ridge about two hours after departing the trailhead. We immediately set up a camera with a long telephoto lens, but were in for a surprise.

Just as we were ready to shoot, the goats bedded down in a spot that made photography difficult. An instant later, on this windswept, over-grazed, bare ridge, a blacktail doe with twin fawns appeared. In a moment these were joined by two spike bucks, possibly the doe's offspring from the previous year. Instead of filming goats on top of the world, we devoted the morning to deer.

Often since then, I have found blacktails in other surprising places. For example, I have found them in soggy mixed forests of Sitka spruce, western red cedar, and big-leaf maple bearded with club moss and lichens. It is surprising that the deer do not grow webbed feet here! Proceeding upslope, I have also encountered blacktails in forests of western white pine as well as silver and Douglas fir. Then I've gone on to such places as Hurricane and Klahhane ridges where the species seemed most abundant of all. If blacktails have one characteristic, it is their adaptability

This shows the blacktail range.

We encountered this blacktail doe and fawn along the trail to Klahhane Ridge in Washington's Olympic National Park. The deer share this windswept high country with mountain goats.

This panorama, looking toward Mount
Olympus from Hurricane Ridge in the
Olympics, is prime blacktail deer
range. This region is typically cloudy
and receives a high annual rainfall,
making it the wettest part of the continental United States.

Blacktail deer thrive in a wide range of habitats along the coasts of the United States and British Columbia, from low elevation rain forests (such as this one along the Hoh River in Washington) to high and drier ridges in the Olympics and the Cascades.

Although blacktail deer did not exist originally on Afognak (in this picture) and Kodiak islands, Alaska, they became well-established after their introduction decades ago. They are now very numerous in both places.

For the record, I have also watched blacktails grazing in dry chaparrals as well as on mountainsides logged clear of timber. Perhaps most remarkable of all, I have intercepted them swimming from Afognak Island, Alaska, where they were successfully stocked long ago, across open channels and inlets to smaller islands. One of these saltwater crossings was over a mile across. But apparently such maritime travel is common thereabouts. My friend, Roy Randall, Afognak Wilderness Lodge owner and guide, reports that he is never surprised even when he finds blacktails on the tiniest offshore islands.

TWO SUBSPECIES

Some taxonomists might question whether blacktails deserve a full chapter in this book. That is, the blacktail is simply a small race or subspecies of mule deer and inhabits the coastal areas of Pacific North America. Actually, what we call the blacktail here is two deer subspecies: the Columbian blacktail (*Odocoileus hemionus columbianus*) and the almost indistinguishable Sitka deer (*O.h. sitkensis*). The Columbian blacktail ranges in a coastal strip from northern California to mainland British Columbia. The smaller Sitka deer ranges from British Columbia's Queen Charlotte Island north through southeastern Alaska to about Yakutat, plus Kodiak and Afognak islands.

By any name or in any habitat, the blacktail looks like a small edition of the mule deer. It has the same jumping gait and, except for the slightly darker coat, is almost the same color. Blacktails and mule deer even hybridize where the ranges

Sitka blacktail deer in Alaska are fair swimmers and readily take to the water. We flushed this one from a small satellite island of Afognak. It readily hit the water and swam to another island about 500 yards away. Blacktails share these islands with Roosevelt elk, also introduced, and brown bears.

overlap. The main difference is that the blacktail has a thin, all-black tail (black on the outside, white underneath), while the mule deer has a black-tipped, all-white tail.

For purposes of trophy record keeping, the Boone and Crockett Club considers blacktail range as being roughly the western third of California, Oregon, Washington, and British Columbia. The blacktail/mule-deer dividing line, with some deviations, is the summit of the Cascade Mountain range in Washington and Interstate Highway 5 in Oregon and California. Deer east of this line are considered mule deer.

Writing in *Outdoor Life* magazine, the experienced Oregonian hunter Dwight Schuh describes blacktails as the wariest of all native deer. He may be correct. My own experience is that they are the hardest to find and photograph. But this may result from my unfamiliarity with the animal and its darker habitat. On average, blacktails tend to live in cover that is denser than that preferred by whitetails and mule deer, and almost any creatures

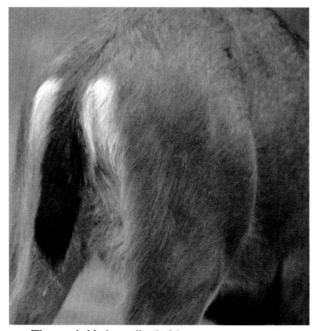

The mostly black, small tail of the blacktail deer distinguishes it from the mule deer, which has a small white tail with a black tip. Mule deer and blacktails do intregrade wherever their ranges overlap.

dwelling in dense, dark places are more difficult to observe than those that spend most of their lives in the open.

The average rack of a blacktail buck isn't as likely to excite as many hunters as an average muley rack would. The typical mature buck of Washington stands three feet at the shoulder and weighs 125 to 135 pounds. The heaviest dressed and authenticated weight for a blacktail deer in Alaska was 212 pounds. Such a buck probably would have tipped honest scales at about 240 or 250 pounds, making it a genuine giant among blacktails.

The Alaskan blacktail deer typically has a reddish-brown coat in summer that is replaced by dark hair in late October. Fully developed antlers on mature bucks are dark, with the same bifurcated pattern (double Y branches on each side) that mule deer have. A mature buck has five points, including the eye guards. Sitka blacktail males simply do not grow heavy antlers. Alaskan blacktails have been known to survive a dozen years, but a lifespan of five or six years is considered a very full one.

Sitka fawns are born in May and June, surprisingly often in the coastal fringe of trees adjacent to lowland muskeg or ocean beach. From birth until they are able to easily follow their mothers, fawns are hunted by wolverines, black bears, grizzly bears, and perhaps bald eagles. The bears are just out of winter hibernation and extremely hungry. Nobody really knows the extent of this predation, but it certainly does not prevent blacktails from being abundant. Wolves are absent from much Sitka deer range, but it is interesting to note that the highest deer populations have occurred where wolves were present. During summer, blacktails migrate upward to browse on alpine ranges free of snow. The first heavy frosts of autumn in turn trigger reverse migration down to the high timber and coastal areas. The rut begins in late October and peaks just before Thanksgiving.

In late summer, this Oregon blacktail, with antlers still in velvet, is bedded in lush tall grass. When its antlers reach full growth (very soon) and the velvet is shed, it will carry an average-size rack for a blacktail.

Black bears have little impact on blacktail populations but in spring will kill adult blacktails weakened by winter starvation as well as fawns the bears happen upon.

Blacktails feed in clear-cut areas, morn-
ings and evenings, where new vegetation is emerging. I flushed this buck
from such a strip, and it raced for the
evergreen forest in the background.

THE RUT

The best time to watch Alaskan blacktails is during the rut when bucks behave as crazily as other deer in America. One November day years ago, Charley Mudd—an itinerant gold miner and brown-bear guide—and I were cruising along a scenic shoreline of Admiralty Island. The day was especially warm, sunny, and calm—a rare combination thereabouts. Taking advantage of a high tide, Charley easily maneuvered his small boat into miniature bays and close to gravel beaches. On rounding one rocky point, we immediately spotted two bucks facing each other on a beach. A third stood nearby, watching the other two. Charley cut the motor and we drifted silently toward the deer.

Necks swollen, the bucks were clearly feeling their oats. One scraped gravel with a front hoof while the other raised and lowered his head, advancing slowly. Suddenly the two were dueling head to head, trying, it seemed, to put one another in the water. Meanwhile, we floated closer and closer. I believe we might actually have drifted to within a few feet without being detected if the bottom of the boat hadn't scraped against gravel.

The noise ended the performance. Startled, all three deer stared at us in disbelief, then bounded away toward the forest behind.

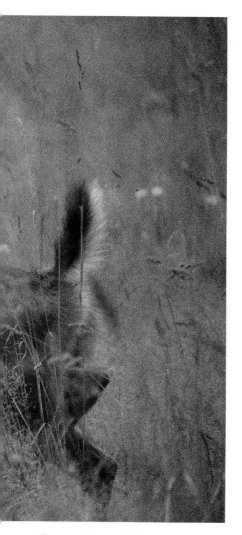

Peggy and I were sitting on the edge of a forest clearing in the foothills of the Cascade Mountains when this black-tail doe approached. She suddenly caught our scent, stopped in indecision, and then pranced away a short distance. She broke into a run a moment after I shot this picture.

"Did you get any pictures?" Charley asked.

I was ashamed to tell him that I had forgotten to use my camera. But since that day long ago, my instincts as a photographer have grown much stronger. Today I would have that blacktail encounter on film.

CALLING BLACKTAILS

Charley Mudd was the first person to show me that North American deer can be called. Blowing on a rubberband stretched between two slivers of wood held in his teeth, Charley several times tempted does and small bucks out of evergreen cover onto the fringe of a beach. Another time he called a doe simply by blowing against a leaf, making a high-pitched sound that he claimed simulated a fawn's cry of distress. Thirty years later I would see Murry Burnham hoodwink a whitetail doe with practically the same sound, 4000 miles away in south Texas.

POPULATION DYNAMICS

When the great Pacific coastal forests were first logged a century or so ago, and forest slashings were created, the blacktail population exploded exactly as any modern biologist could have predicted. A lot of the deer were soon being shot for subsistence. Until a certain mineral lick in California's Trinity National Forest was made a sanctuary in 1911, commercial hunters shot an estimated 10,000 deer in that vicinity.

Today, regulated hunting is not making a dent in blacktail populations. But growing competition from livestock definitely does. Sheep and domestic goats, for example, compete for almost all of the same foods that blacktails prefer. The conflict with cattle is not quite so serious. But it is quite clear that blacktails become few and far between in areas where sheep raising goes on. Anyway, intense sheep grazing too often leaves an area unfit for other use.

Alaskan deer populations fluctuate with the severity of the winters. A rigorous winter or—worse—a series of them can reduce deer herds to low levels. But, as with whitetails and mule deer, blacktails have a high reproductive potential and their numbers rebuild rapidly when bad winters are followed by normal or mild winters.

In winter the deer concentrate below the snow-line, which means in a zone not too far from the coastlines. The bucks that lose the most weight and energy during the rut have the most difficulty surviving. If the hunger moon is prolonged, the bucks and the fawns of the previous spring are most likely to perish. Or, weakened, they are the ones most likely to be caught by bruins coming out of hibernation. Charley Mudd once told me that bear hunting was best along isolated beaches wherever he knew or figured there would be a winter deer kill.

FOOD

During the rainy and sometimes short coastal summers, food for the blacktails is abundant and of good quality. In spring deer utilize the new green shoots of beach grasses, sedges, and plantain. But with the onset of summer they eat mainly herbaceous plants. As snow recedes up the mountainsides, blacktails browse on skunk cabbage, marsh marigold, and blueberry and salmonberry leaves. By July and into August, deer cabbage is the main food. Following early frosts, southeastern Alaskan deer gorge heavily on young shoots of salmonberry and black currant as they travel down through heavy timber and alder slides. With the onslaught of winter, deer must turn more and more to woody plants. They will eventually lose weight on such a diet, and may be forced to eat beach grass (now dry and devoid of nutrition) and kelp that has washed ashore. The quality of these foods is low, and biologists have actually examined deer that were starving despite having full stomachs.

Blacktails are surprisingly good climbers, and in Washington and on Vancouver Island I have watched them feed along sheer rock ledges where it was too hazardous for me to follow. Perhaps they performed such acrobatics to reach favored plants. At least, it did not seem necessary for them to be in such precipitous places for any other reason. I have also seen them dig up mushrooms, and maybe roots or bulbs as well, with their hooves. During springtime blacktails will wade readily into shallow water to nibble on new growth of musk or water parsley.

Blacktails sometimes eat skunk cabbage. Alaskan blacktails especially relish the tender young shoots. Bears like the plant even better.

Elderberries brighten up some corners
of the landscape where blacktails live.
Deer prefer the leaves, not berries.

HABITAT AND BURNS

Although Alaskan blacktails may not be the
most magnificent of our deer, they certainly do live
in the most magnificent land. That is the dividend,
the bonus, for anyone who seeks them on misty
islands or stormy seacoasts. This may be the most
spectacular deer habitat on earth.

Anybody looking for the more southern, Columbian blacktails is wise to turn his attention to
burn areas. In recent years, perhaps taking a clue
from old Indian accounts, the California Department of Fish and Game (along with the U.S. Forest
Service in some areas) has been creating new habitat
and improving worn-out habitat through controlled burning. Of course, fire was an old Indian
drive-hunting technique. But the Indians also knew

that the bright green vegetation sprouting in old burns attracted deer. So if you want to find blacktails, you might try burn areas.

Here's how it works: Blacktails are browsers, and climax forests offer little browse in the understory for deer. The second-growth brush that follows a timber cutting often does not offer much valuable nutrition either. But burn this brush to the ground and new growth bursts forth. Blacktails do not need invitations to move into burn areas. In fact, they have been observed moving into burned areas while the ashes and undergrowth were still smouldering. This may be an unconscious need for suddenly available minerals.

Not every fire is a good one. For example, a fire that's too hot only sterilizes the ground. But fire management technicians have reduced burning almost to an art. Managers have learned to wait for very humid days when old brush will burn, but still not bake the topsoil. One plant that follows proper blazes in California is *ceanothus*, locally called buckbrush, which unfortunately is a common name for many other unrelated plants all over the West. This high-protein evergreen shrub is said to be as nourishing as alfalfa hay, and deer depend on it, particu-

larly during midwinter. Buckbrush is one of those plants that actually needs fire to survive, because the seed casings do not break open until they are scorched.

The feeding habits of blacktail deer are interesting and worth describing for a number of reasons. First, they browse in a manner that seems designed to best preserve their own habitat. On Vancouver Island, British Columbia, where the blacktail population is large, these feeding habits have been studied carefully through all seasons. The deer tend to browse uphill, usually on different kinds of plants instead of concentrating on the most palatable growths. They also concentrate on the underside or downhill side of dense thickets, rather than vice versa, which is good for soil conservation. Blacktails also feed around the margins of dense clumps of vegetation, rather than forcing their way into them. That way the heavy natural cover is not depleted. By comparison, domestic stock would quickly deplete the same area.

When feeding, a blacktail can reach up to about 50 inches from the ground. Overbrowsing occurs when deer have eaten all cover over a significant area—revealed by a definite browse line up to

50 inches high. Such lines let biologists know that there are too many deer for the carrying capacity of the range.

Browsing blacktails can also inflict damage on young forests, particularly on clear-cut areas that have been newly planted. The large timber companies have spent much money researching means of keeping deer from young plantations. To date, none of the deterrent measures have worked very well.

In some areas blacktails have a hard time re-sisting the bounty they find in orchards, vineyards, farmlands, and gardens. Judging from what I once saw in an Oregon garden, planted on the edge of a forest, these coastal deer must be mad for tulips, delphiniums, and strawberries. In some areas, gardeners need deer-proof fences to protect carrots, turnips, peas, lettuce, and Brussels sprouts.

So long as we do not cut down all the Pacific forests, pollute the Alaskan beaches, and mine the lonely and spectacular fiords, we will probably have plenty of blacktail deer.

Here, two immature blacktails browse in Olympic National Park. Blacktails are the most difficult of our native deer to photograph, owing to their shyness and the often dimly lit environment.

An encounter with a blacktail buck often means seeing only a shadow or silhouette moving silently through the woods. Your chances for finding and spotting blacktails improve after a snowfall.

CHAPTER 4
DEER BEHAVIORS

Early one clear, subfreezing November morning in Livingston County, Michigan, Bill Pruitt was watching over a salt block that had been placed where an oak-hickory woods adjoined a grassy meadow. This was a good time and good place to observe whitetail deer. Soon Pruitt saw a handsome 8-point buck of about 225 pounds come to the edge of the timber. There the animal stopped and rattled its antlers against low-hanging oak limbs, while uttering low grunts. Next, wrote Pruitt in the February 1953 issue of *Journal of Mammology*, the deer "reached up and grasped oak limbs in its mouth, pulled them down, and by twisting his head, raked his antlers through them.

"Alternating with this activity were spells when the buck pawed the ground with its forefeet, throwing soil and leaves up over its back, and raked its antlers, first one side, then the other, through the leaves and loose soil.

"Occasionally the buck would wheel in a circle, flash his flag, grunt, and then resume his antler rattling and pawing. The whole procedure was reminiscent of a domestic bull when he smells a cow in heat or is working himself into a frenzy to make a charge."

The buck continued this activity for ten minutes before finally moving closer to Pruitt along the edge of the woods. Head and swollen neck outthrust, still shaking its antlers and grunting, the buck eventually caught human scent and disappeared. No other deer were in sight during the buck's entire performance.

As manifestation of the rut, this fat muley buck seems to be taking on an entire alder thicket, rattling his antlers noisily in the dry, bare branches. Three other bucks of similar size had gathered in this immediate area.

This muley buck is engaged in a violent battle with a bush. In the process, the buck also dug up the ground and urinated on its feet. When I filmed this activity, in late November, there were no other deer in sight to be impressed.

Pruitt inspected the area after the buck departed and found that the buck had left a pawed circle about three feet in diameter. All fallen brown leaves were scraped away. The soil was broken and trampled—with hoof and antler marks deeply imprinted. Continuing Pruitt's description: "Loose soil was scattered for several feet around the circle on top of the leaf litter. No evidence of fresh urine was noted. The lower limbs of the tree immediately over the circle were torn, scarred (barked), and broken."

THE RUT

Deer behavior may seem strange and unpredictable, if not unfathomable at any time of year, but it is never more interesting than during the rut of late fall. What Pruitt had witnessed was fairly typical—a buck making a scrape—but with a few added antics.

Anyone who spends enough time in a deer woods during the rut may be fortunate enough to see something similar, or something even more bizarre. I once watched a mule deer buck on the edge of a hayfield raking up big clumps of hay with its antlers, exactly like a rancher wielding a pitchfork, and then violently tossing them away. When finally finished, the buck left a circular area of bare earth compacted with hundreds of hoofprints. In this instance, too, no other deer was in sight. The buck seemed to be performing for its own pleasure, or rage, or relief.

The rut or rutting season is that frenetic or hyperactive period when male deer are capable of breeding. Although whitetail bucks in North America (particularly in New York and the Northeast) have successfully bred from September to February, a span of six months, most does are successfully bred during a period that lasts only two to four weeks, with each doe receptive only about 30 hours. This could be termed the peak of the rut, and occurs toward the end of autumn.

On the average, and with numerous exceptions, deer of northern latitudes tend to breed earlier than deer farther south. For example, in the Washington Puget Sound area, the high point of the blacktail rut usually comes in early October. For whitetails in south and west Texas, it often falls during the Christmas holidays or even later. Although factors such as weather and genetics may influence timing of the rut, the exact breeding date depends much more on two other factors: range conditions and a process called *photoperiodism*.

Here is how photoperiodism works. The decreasing daylight of autumn stimulates a deer's

This mule deer has reduced a small bush almost to stubble with its antlers, the demolition possibly due to frustration. A buck with antlers twice as heavy had monopolized a nearby doe. Later I watched the same buck dig up another shrub.

pituitary gland through its eyes. The pituitary gland manufactures and releases increasing amounts of those hormones that stimulate both male and female sex glands to a peak of activity. That is when we see deer behaving more dramatically than at any other time. For deer, this is the most exciting time of the year.

The sex life, which is really the *secret* sex life to most observers, is not only fascinating; it can also give any deer observer leads on getting closer to deer. When bucks shed their antler velvet, and for a time thereafter, they leave behind much sign, such as damage to saplings and brush, and scraped bark on small trees. This is very easy to see but does not mean that the buck is still in the vicinity. But if you find a pawed-out scrape or scrapes like those described earlier, an eager buck is probably nearby.

Time and again during the peak of the rut, I have watched both mule and whitetail bucks traveling almost aimlessly, in broad daylight, in search of receptive does. This, of all times, is when males are

Damage such as this on low trees results from antler rubs. If ground scrapes are fresh, the buck *may* be in the area. Or the fresh scrape may only indicate a buck has passed through.

Here is a good example of a deer rub on a sapling. Even more positive proof of the buck's continued presence nearby would be a fresh hoof scraping on the ground. You can usually detect a urine odor in the dirt if the scrape is fresh enough.

least cautious of humans. During these travels, a buck will occasionally pause and scrape out a patch of ground, sometimes very small, sometimes an area big enough in which to pitch a pup tent. He may or may not urinate on the spot, but he usually does. There is considerable disagreement as to whether the scrapes are made simply at random as the buck searches or whether the scrapes are territorial and meant to warn other bucks away. Either way, a scrape is an open invitation to any and all estrus does in the area. This advertising seems to pay off, too.

At daybreak one morning in December, from a tower blind in the south-Texas brush country, I watched a fine 12-point whitetail buck make a scrape on the edge of a sendero, a swath ranchers had cut through dense vegetation with a mechanical brush hog. Later that same day, and for two days following, the same buck returned at intervals to enlarge his scrape. At least three other bucks also checked the spot, but didn't linger long. A doe and

fawn also came, but neither even stopped feeding except to stare briefly at me in the tower. A passing coyote was only slightly more interested.

Early on the fourth afternoon, and not far from that spot, I found a cluster of scrapes in a fairly small area and decided to take a stand near that site the next morning. I arrived well before dawn and waited, motionless, until the sun was well above the horizon and very warm on my back. No deer appeared. Checking out the cluster of scrapes, however, I discovered that they had been almost obliterated. Sometime during the interval, probably after dark, at least two and maybe several deer had thoroughly trampled the ground all around the area, tearing up brush in the process. There were a number of different-size hoofprints as well. I have no idea whether combat or breeding or both had taken place, but there must have been one lively encounter.

Late one summer in Oregon's Siskiyou National Forest, ranger Robert M. Clark was walking

The number of hoofprints and their freshness are always a rough index of deer numbers in any area. But deer can suddenly vanish from any area. The very large and largest hoofprints are usually made by bucks.

homeward down a long logging road. Suddenly he heard crashing metal and hurried toward the sound. Quickly he found a car, which somebody had parked beside an open glade, under violent attack. A blacktail buck circled nearby and at intervals would slash at the auto with its antlers. When Clark approached, the deer was startled and raced away.

On closer inspection Clark found one door of the car badly dented and punctured. He also saw his own face mirrored in the polished surface. From that he concluded that the buck also saw itself mirrored as a rival deer and was trying to drive itself away.

Clark witnessed another strange deer incident when he worked as a forest officer in Montana's Lolo National Forest. Returning from a timber sale in autumn he decided to take a shortcut back to his camp along a deer trail. En route he heard the unmistakable sounds of deer conflict: scraping, hoof pounding, antler rattling not far away. Stalking closer he found four, not just two bucks engaged in an unusual tournament.

Two of the bucks were large and two were smaller. All were fighting. At first the fight mainly concerned the two larger bucks, thrusting at one another head to head. But the smaller ones took turns trying to join the struggle. According to Clark the bout lasted about 20 minutes and ended when one of the large bucks broke away, lunged savagely at a small one, and drove it running full speed into the forest. The others then drifted away.

Pellets, or droppings, are among the most visible deer sign. Popular bedding areas usually have numerous and closely grouped pellet piles.

BREEDING

A whitetail doe is receptive to breeding for about a day and a night. Before that time she leaves behind an aura of estrus which a buck, and probably more than one, is certain to scent. This buck, or contingent of bucks, follows the female until she is finally receptive. The breeder, if only one, is the winner of any bluffing matches or outright fighting that takes place. Even a huge and powerful buck suffers a constant, enervating struggle to remain the number-one stud throughout the rut.

Studies revealed that if a doe is not bred during that first estrus, which is extremely rare even in areas where the doe-to-buck ratio is very high, the female will come into estrus again 28 days later. According to some biologists, that doe can even come into estrus a third time if necessary. So, although barren does can possibly exist on good deer range when winter gives way to spring, they are oddities. Normally, healthy female deer produce fawns each year as long as they live.

Recent research at Auburn University in Alabama has shown that does are greatly assured of meeting bucks during the rut. By equipping both male and female whitetails with radio-transmitter collars, biologists have observed that during the rut bucks almost double their travels and normal ranges of about 220 acres. At the same time, the collared does slightly decreased their daily wanderings. This seemed to help the roaming bucks find the receptive does.

This mule deer doe is in estrus, and during the hour or so that I watched, the buck followed her relentlessly. Twice the male had to bluff other smaller bucks away, but they did not retreat too far. Commonly this pursuit may continue for two days or longer, as the doe's aura persists.

This muley buck is on the trail of a doe just out of the picture. As I watched, a buck with much heavier antlers abruptly ended the romance for our subject. The intimidated buck remained in the vicinity though, in case.

SCRAPES

Back briefly to scrapes and scraping, which are so important if you are searching for deer: Blacktails tend to make scrapes in dense, dark places, often where several deer trails converge in an evergreen woods. Mule deer are apt to make scrapes anywhere, although I have found many of their scrapes in the bottoms of dry draws and along streambeds where the water flow had been reduced to a trickle. Whitetail bucks scrape near forest openings or edges. In the Midwest, these may be where woodlots adjoin cropfields. One Minnesota researcher considered swamp edges good places to look. Veteran Florida outdoor writer Charley Dickey notes that southern deer often make scrapes beneath live oaks and water oaks, while at the same time chewing off twigs just above the scrapes.

There is no point in wasting time on stand, watching an old or abandoned scrape. On the other hand, bucks will regularly return to fresh ones. One way to tell if a scrape is old or fresh is to run your fingers through the earth. If it is dry and odorless, it's probably old; but if it's damp and smells of urine, it's active. More than likely the scraper is within a half mile of the scrape.

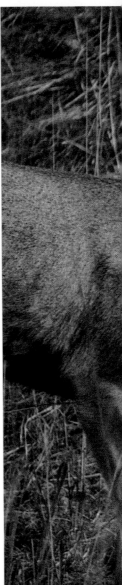

I first saw these two mule deer bucks feeding directly toward one another in northwestern Wyoming. So I set up a camera with a long telephoto lens on a tripod, and aimed where they might meet. Luckily, they met at that spot and even had a bout that lasted a few seconds to decide right-of-way.

HUNTING VS. THE RUT

Because the rutting season and open hunting seasons often coincide all across the continent, some obvious questions arise. Can hunting pressure alter the normal rut? Can hunting cause a herd to be less productive? Can hunting lead to an imbalance in the buck-doe ratio, and therefore leave too few bucks to service the does? The answer to all three questions is *no*. In some states where hunting is traditional during the rut, deer herds have still become too large for their range. In fact, limited research has shown that more male fawns may be born in heavily hunted areas.

From a bluff overlooking an Idaho stream at a livestock crossing and watering place, I noticed many deer tracks mingled in with those of the cattle. Several days later this buck arrived to take a drink.

In my experience, deer tend to use the same trails day after day and year after year unless or until something happens to disrupt the habit. This trail through a marshy area in Ohio connects two hardwood ridges. Whitetails traveling between the two areas used this same path the entire four years I observed it.

POPULATION AND HABITAT

The greatest lasting damage to a deer herd and its habitat could come from not harvesting enough doe deer to keep the herd within the carrying capacity of the range. Any range can support only so many deer in good health. Beyond that the condition of the deer deteriorates. All North American deer are polygamous, and an individual buck can and will mate with many females during a breeding season. In a captive herd in the Adirondacks, one buck was known to have impregnated 19 females. In areas where the range is not overcrowded and where the buck-doe ratio is fairly close to even, deer almost invariably grow to larger size, and the bucks develop more impressive antlers. In fact, that is a major conclusion of Texas biologists Al Brothers and Murphy Ray in their important book on deer management, *Producing Quality Whitetails*.

CHOICE OF RANGE

The movements of deer have always been a mystery, or at least have been very baffling. At certain times of the year all species of American deer do live fairly predictable lives. For example, I have known large mule deer bucks to spend an entire summer in a high mountain glen, little larger than 100 acres. The deer never seemed to move beyond the perimeter, and we could usually find them there without difficulty. Come autumn, however, and the deer simply vanished. What happened to these bucks after heavy snows began to fall is anybody's guess.

Another good example of unpredictable movement is the old muley buck that lived for several

This mule deer trail is both a migration route from summer to winter range, and a path used for daily trips from bedding (on a steep slope) to feeding areas. Summer backpackers use the same pathway to reach the Wyoming backcountry.

It is not unusual for a deer that feels concealed to sit tight rather than flush when approached. This tactic succeeds far more often than people realize.

With the rut over, the necks of these Montana mule deer bucks are no longer swollen. They have formed a bachelor herd on a snow-free wintering area. In late spring they will ascend to the snow-covered mountains.

summers in the Grant Village Campground at Yellowstone National Park. Campers could see the deer almost every day. He posed for thousands of photographers among the tents and recreational vehicles. But when the campground was closed for the season in late September, the buck disappeared, and didn't return until May. Where it wandered during that period is one of those mysteries. At least it was not shot by hunters if its travels carried it outside park boundaries, which is probably the case. Any large animal would have a hard time wintering where snow sometimes accumulates to eight feet deep, as it does for many miles around that Grant Village campground.

I watched this buck reach the edge of the woods and pause there. It appeared anxious to join other deer feeding in a grainfield, but it was hesitant. The buck stomped its hoofs several times— a typical behavior showing doubt— before walking stiffly into the open.

A wild whitetail's wariness is counteracted, at times, only by its curiosity. This doe ran the instant she saw me, but when I sat down she stopped and peered back above the vegetation. Without moving more than absolutely necessary, I shot the picture.

HOW WEATHER AFFECTS ACTIVITY

Dave Morris, a Georgia outdoor writer and editor, has collected some revealing facts about whitetail movements and weather on a 14,000-acre hunting club preserve in Georgia, to which he belongs. Whitetails on the preserve are not pursued too heavily during the open hunting season, and the animals remain relatively undisturbed for the balance of the year. For a number of years Morris kept records of deer activity, or rather of the amount of deer activity, during different kinds of atmospheric conditions and temperatures. Roughly, here is what he found.

Deer movement was consistently higher when the temperature for a particular day of the year was normal or below normal. This deer activity was also evenly distributed throughout the day. But on days with above-normal temperatures, deer traveled much more in the morning than later on.

The effect of barometric pressure on everything from bears to brown trout has been studied for a long time and the results are not in agreement. However, there is a correlation between activity level and a high barometer. Morris concluded that even if barometric pressure itself does not affect deer behavior, the weather systems (or symptoms?)

accompanying it are indeed important. His southeastern deer were much more active with a barometric pressure hovering about 29.00 inches than below that figure. At the same time, Morris knows that deer activity averaged much higher when the humidity was low. Movement slowed noticeably during periods of fog, haze, and rain (all high-humidity situations), and the longer these conditions lasted the more secretive the deer became.

THE MOON

Even more mysterious and confusing than the effects of weather is the moon's influence on deer movement. Solid statistics are lacking on this, simply because it is hard to observe animals at night and the laws in many states discourage people from wandering around a deer woods after dark, a time when poachers do most of their work.

Morris believes that his Georgia whitetails move much more than normal during early morning and late evening on a new moon. My old friend, Larry Moore, a great mule deer guide of Jackson Hole, believed the same was true of mule deer where he hunted in the Hoback-Granite Creek area of northwestern Wyoming. On a new moon he would be out and high up on the slopes by daybreak. During a full or old moon, he would eat a more leisurely breakfast and hit the trail later.

PLAY

When the land is green and lush, healthy deer of all ages engage in what we might call "play," but which is really something else. I have watched both fawns and adults chasing and jumping over one another, wheeling, leaping, gamboling, and butting each other like children gathered on a playground. This behavior begins among fawns as soon as they are old enough to come out of hiding and run at high speeds. There are at least two possible explanations for this play.

In winter deer of colder, more northern latitudes grow longer hair than southern deer. If there is sufficient food and a deer does not spend too much energy foraging, it can usually survive the most bitter of winters without difficulty.

Both mule deer, like this one, and whitetails are active at night. They move confidently through the dark and are less afraid of humans then. This photo, made with a flash, helps convey why poachers operate so effectively after sundown.

These three does were surprised out in an open forest glade. One of them is practically airborne in its swift dash to the protective cover of the woods.

A whitetail deer has many escape mechanisms, perhaps the most important being its speed afoot. A frightened deer can disappear in a surprisingly short time. It can bound over obstacles almost as easily as it can run across flat terrain.

Some biologists see deer play as an index of environmental conditions. They reason that this activity could indicate an excess of energy, which reflects the general good physical condition of the animals. For comparison, healthy human children tend to play more vigorously and for longer periods than sluggish or undernourished children. It seems to be true that deer play more where the population density is low and the quality of the habitat is high. When deer fill their range to capacity, or during years when forage is in short supply, they spend less time playing and more time foraging. Playing consequently may be a sign that all is well with the local deer herd.

Another, and perhaps better, explanation for deer play is that it is training and conditioning for a longer life, in fact for survival. Running and jumping stimulates and builds stronger muscles and develops lung capacity. The same maneuvers a deer uses in apparent play can later help it escape from predators. Cougar cubs instinctively stalk and spring on one another, which provides practice for killing later on. And young mule deer jump and dash around, developing the abilities to escape cougars in sudden, life-or-death encounters.

Mule deer seem to play less than whitetails, and whitetails play less and less as they mature. Older adult bucks play very little or not at all. This play usually starts and stops suddenly, as if on some silent signal. One biologist believes this is a vigilance measure, in that a deer can better detect approaching danger by stopping suddenly. The cessation is somewhat similar to that of a night burglar's when he is suddenly illuminated.

AGGRESSION

Although many people think of deer as shy or playful, deer can be highly aggressive. According to Canadian wildlife biologist Valerius Geist, who has studied blacktail deer (*Mule and Blacktail Deer of North America*), "aggression is behavior by which individual animals create and maintain access to scarce resources against the actions of conspecific competitors. It is active competition in which one individual, in some fashion, displaces another." By *conspecific*, Geist means an animal of the same species. And by scarce resources, he means food, living space or room, and sexual partners.

Competition for food is most intense, if it exists at all, during winter when the range is in poor condition, or during serious, prolonged drought. Anybody who has spent time in a northern winter deer "yard," where food is very limited, has seen the fierce competition among deer for the limited,

The more deer in a group, the more likely that conflict occurs. This clash between does, probably over food, is typical. They face off, rise on hind legs, and slash at one another with front hoofs. In such contests, I have never seen damage inflicted.

and usually diminishing, food supply. Large bucks kick and drive smaller does away. And does attack their own fawns to keep them at a distance. At times some of the weakest eventually starve to death. Only the fittest, strongest, and most aggressive survive the most severe periods.

The most noticeable competition for living space occurs in spring when the dominant, oldest, or largest does obtain the most secure sites for dropping their fawns and for finding abundant food in the vicinity. Clashes observed between female mule deer at this time are almost certainly over the best fawning areas.

I have already covered aggressive behavior in the rut. Bucks confront one another for does in estrus by every means from subtle threats to overt enforcement with antlers. More than once Peggy and I have also seen does clash at this time. On one occasion, in northern Wyoming, we saw a muley doe, coming into estrus, being closely trailed by a sleek, heavy buck, tongue out and breathing heavily. A second female appeared and innocently strolled close to the first. When the intruder came too near, the first doe reared onto her hind legs and drove away her rival with flailing front hoofs. Apparently every deer at some time will show extreme annoyance, if not downright aggression, toward other deer. On the average, though, deer are still much more compatible than humans.

DANGEROUS TO MAN?

On a November morning, 1977, in Yosemite National Park, Colin Neu, age five, was feeding potato chips to a young mule deer buck when the semi-tame animal suddenly snatched away the whole bag. The boy tried to grab it back, and the deer pinned the child to the ground and killed him.

That Yosemite tragedy was no freak. Deer that have become familiar with and highly accustomed to people can become very aggressive toward people for the same reasons they are aggressive toward other deer. Children are not the only vicitms. Deer

I was apprehensive about this deer. It was raised from birth around a ranchhouse rather than in the wild. As it grew it became very familiar and comfortable with people. During the autumn rut it behaved aggressively enough to deserve cautious watching.

have also killed human adults and dogs. According to California biologist Jack White, a Napa County man who made a hobby of raising deer, entered a pen one rainy night to feed his pet buck and was promptly attacked. Somehow the man managed to reach his kitchen telephone before collapsing and dying. His wounds were so terrible that investigators at first suspected he had been a victim of a ritual murder.

There is no substantiated record that a completely wild, healthy, uninjured North American deer has ever attacked a human without provocation. Hunters have been attacked while approaching crippled or stunned deer. In fact, several hunters have been killed that way. But deer that have become accustomed to people should be regarded with caution. Photographers, especially, should use care.

One autumn day in 1980, cameraman Kim Heller of Ohio's Division of Wildlife was "shooting" a captive buck on a private game farm. The animal lunged at Heller and gored him. He died several days later.

Several years ago I stood by as a Columbus, Ohio, newspaper photographer was filming deer in a 100-acre enclosure. He had taken along his 4-year-old son, who wanted to see the deer. As I watched the photographer approach the buck, I saw the animal focus its attention on the little boy, who was toddling behind. Suddenly the deer rushed the boy,

who stumbled or was pushed into a fence corner. That fence saved the boy's life, because the deer caught its antlers in the woven wire and could not thrust them into the child. I had to drive away the deer with a club.

Commercial petting-park deer are potentially dangerous, especially in the fall. In Baltimore a tame deer escaped from a humane society compound and attacked a middle-aged couple walking along the street.

Ron Schara, outdoor editor of the *Minneapolis Tribune*, was scouting a woods prior to the opening

It is often written that deer do not look upward, supposedly because they do not anticipate danger overhead. Deer *do* look up, but infrequently. So an elevated position is a good vantage for observing deer.

of bowhunting season. Without warning, Schara was attacked by a deer, and he has scars on his arm to prove it. He thought it was the first authentic unprovoked attack by a wild, healthy deer, but later learned that it was a captive-raised animal that had recently been released into the wild.

One day a friend brought Hugh Codding of Santa Rosa, California, a five-year-old mule deer buck that had been raised in captivity. Against the advice of the local game warden, Codding (who had some knowledge of wildlife from years of hunting) decided to keep the deer in a small lot by his home.

This turned out to be a grave mistake. One day the buck suddenly attacked a hired woodcutter who was using a chainsaw. Then the buck attacked Codding's son David and finally Codding himself, bloodying all three. After the deer was shot, Codding concluded that picking up a fawn and keeping it captive is, at the very least, signing its death warrant, and maybe your own as well.

A word of caution should be sufficient. We know much about the behavior of North American deer, true. But there is also much, much more we do *not* know.

CHAPTER 5
ANTLERS

For generations, the growth, purpose, and beauty of deer antlers have stimulated conversation and argument around campfires, in cozy clubhouses, and in antiseptic laboratories. Interest becomes greater every year. Hunters dream of bagging a buck that's bigger than any other, and photographers yearn to see one in the viewfinder. I know, because I have spent countless hours in the search. Someday I'll snap the shutter on my super buck, but I had better do it no later than late December. After that the antlers will be shed and lost, probably in some remote place where no man will find them.

Shed antlers seldom last long in the wild, although they do survive much longer than the time it takes to grow them. As storehouses of several mineral salts, they are soon nibbled upon by mice, rats, squirrels, porcupines, and other creatures.

Antlers that are not eaten will eventually be bleached white, softened, and weathered away by the elements until they become part of the soil. The minerals in every shed antler will provide nutrients for plants, which in turn will be eaten by deer that will grow new antlers. Thus antlers illustrate well the eternal recycling in nature.

This West Texas whitetail sports an extraordinarily large set of antlers for his tender age of three and a half. To see how large his antlers became two annual sets of antlers later, study the next group of photos.

BIG CHARLIE

In late 1979 newspapers across Texas ran a strange obituary, not for some local politician or dignitary but for a whitetail buck named Big Charlie. Big Charlie died of "natural causes" at the age of six and a half, just before Christmas at the Kerr Wildlife Management Area where he had spent his entire life. Charlie was a handsome, better-than-average buck who had sired 32 offspring, half of them male, but his fame and obituary stem from another reason. Texans have a considerable interest in their deer, and biologists may have learned more about the role of genetics in deer antler development from Charlie than from any other buck.

According to biologist Donnie Harmel, only one of Charlie's male offspring was a spike buck (with a single tine making up each antler) when one and a half years old. All other of Charlie's offspring had more tines. In comparison, almost half of the

All photos in this grouping are of the same buck as in the previous captioned photo except that here he is five-and-a-half years old and his antlers would now class him as a "super" buck—a perfect 10-pointer, with massive beams that are almost symmetrical. Adequate range, genetics, and nutrition are keys to producing bucks such as this. For these photos, deer had been attracted with bait consisting of corn and sweet potatoes. And I used a 600mm lens.

bucks sired by other bucks at Kerr were only spikes at the same age. Obviously Charlie was siring big young bucks whose antlers developed sooner than normal.

The bottom line is that spike bucks are really inferior animals of inferior lineage, and that they will never grow up to sport the kind of trophy racks that make whitetail bucks the most beautiful animals in the world. From Charlie's offspring, we now have proof that a yearling buck that has been sired by a healthy father, and that is living in good range with good nutrition, can grow at least fork horns and perhaps more during its second summer. On several occasions my friend Hefner Appling has taken me out on his Senderos Ranch in south Texas and shown me strong, sleek bucks with eight points—four to the side—that were only one and a half years old. These deer were destined to become the most magnificent of bucks.

This Texas whitetail, which is one and a half years old, is just a spike buck but should have forked antlers or even three points on each antler at his age. But this buck is probably genetically inferior and living on an overcrowded range or both.

This mule deer has typical (symmetrical) antlers for the species—four points per side, forming two Ys. The so-called trophy bucks tend to have much heavier antler beams, however.

TROPHY ANTLERS

Perhaps no aspect of native North American deer is so fascinating or so often discussed and debated as antler growth and development. In many a club and community across the United States, a man was and is known for the size of the deer antlers hanging over the fireplace. If his name happens to be in the Boone & Crockett record book, so much the better. Collecting a large trophy deer with a magnificent rack—either on film or to be mounted—certainly can be a result of pure luck. But far more often it denotes that the hunter is a skilled woodsman who knows his outdoors as well as his living room.

I photographed this fine whitetail in August, in velvet with antlers still growing, in the same general area as the super buck shown at the beginning of this chapter. This one is probably related to the super buck, and since it is young it also may in another year or two develop much more.

HORNS VS. ANTLERS

Although we now know much about antlers and antler growth, a good many mysteries and misconceptions remain. For instance, there is confusion between horns and antlers.

Any horn has a bony center, or core, surrounded by a hardened covering called keratin, which grows all during the animal's life. Keratin is also present in hair, hoofs, fingernails, beaks, claws, and even armadillo shells and snakeskins. Livestock, bighorn sheep, mountain goats, kudus, gazelles, and many other quadrupeds have horns. Of these horned species, both males and females have horns, although the males' tend to be larger. Our native pronghorn antelope also grows horns, but the horns are slightly out of the ordinary. The pronghorn sheds the outer keratin sheath after the breeding season every fall; other horned animals do not shed at all.

In contrast to horns, antlers consist of solid bone. Antlers are also deciduous, which means they are shed and new ones are grown each year. Only members of the deer family have these outgrowths of the skeletal system, primarily composed of calcium, phosphorus, and other minerals. In the New World this family includes elk, moose, caribou, introduced reindeer, and of course mule deer, whitetails, blacktails, and exotic deer. With the exception of caribou and reindeer, only the males grow antlers. Moose grow the largest, heaviest antlers, and a rare moose rack or two from Alaska has been measured at more than seven feet wide. This growth is astounding when you consider that this great mass developed in only a few months' time. But the antler growth of a large male deer is no less astounding because the deer may be only a fourth or fifth the size of a mature moose. A deer's main antler beams are known to have grown about half an inch per day!

A healthy deer begins to grow a fresh set of antlers in the spring, either just before or about the same time that fawns are born. From the moment new antlers grow out from pedicels on the deer's skull, they are covered with aptly named "velvet" until they stop growing in early fall. How fast and to what size the antlers grow depends, as noted earlier, on heredity and nutrition. For example, Big Charlie's antlers grew to great size and so did those of his offspring.

Antler velvet, a furry substance that somewhat resembles brown suede, is a pigmented epidermis of fine hairs—an extension of the skin. It bleeds freely if cut, bruises fairly easily, and suffers from frostbite if retained on the hard antler too late in the fall. This condition no doubt explains why a buck still in the velvet remains fairly docile and even seems to protect his covered antlers from harm. A serious injury results in a deformed set of antlers, with the deformity perhaps lasting forever. But as soon as the velvet is gone, a buck evidences a sudden change of personality.

Deer velvet has always tickled the human imagination. At least some American Indians hunted late summer deer for two primary reasons. The meat was fat and prime at that time, true. But, like some Orientals, the Indians believed that the velvet was an aphrodisiac. That fond hope still lingers, and today there are scattered deer (and elk) farms that raise animals for the velvet alone. The antlers are sawed off, for sale, before the velvet is shed.

Antlers grow from June through August almost everywhere in North America. By September or, at the latest, October, the antlers are fully mineralized—hardened—under the velvet. The hormone balance in a buck's body then changes and the blood supply to the antlers is cut off. No longer nourished, the velvet dies and begins to peel away. During this period I have seen bucks moving about with shreds of dried black or dark-red velvet hanging from their racks. Blood sometimes oozes around the pedicels, and the lower antlers are briefly stained bright red. Go out in good deer range in early fall and you may see bucks rubbing off the last of the velvet on brush and saplings. I am convinced that the biggest bucks dispose of their velvet before the smaller bucks do.

I shot this close-up of a South Dakota whitetail in velvet in early summer. It is likely that this buck developed an impressive rack by the rutting season.

These two photos show a fine Texas whitetail sporting 14 points, including one drop point that was broken off in a fight before the photos were made. Note the relationships of antler and body size.

ANTLER COLORATION

I have seen antlers of every color from ivory to dark mahogany. The coloration comes from two sources: stain received from hemoglobin of the blood in the velvet, and somewhat less from stains in the bark on which the antlers were rubbed. Any stain gradually vanishes from the antlers, as it is bleached or washed out by sunlight and rain.

From my lifetime of watching deer, it appears to me that the darker the antlers, the older the buck is likely to be. This is not an infallible rule, but it is true much of the time. Here's why: Velvet is stripped from some bucks while there is still a supply of blood in the tissue, while the velvet hangs onto other antlers until dry. The antlers with a good blood supply will consequently be stained darker, especially when you consider that large antlers have bigger, more extensive blood vessels than small ones. A buck with a large and heavy rack will thus probably have more blood stain, particularly on the main beams near the base.

If you vagabond long enough in mule deer country, especially in alpine elevations until late autumn, when snow and the rut drive deer downward, you may come upon a handsome Wyoming buck such as this one. Reaching such places demands sturdy hiking shoes, a backpack, and a willingness to hike steep, rocky trails.

This is a remarkable and very old whitetail buck. Its age is not known, but it has 17 total points from two widespread main beams, including one drop point. It possibly had an even larger rack the year or two before I made these pictures in the south Texas brush country. Unfortunately, the deer was shot for his antlers by night poachers. The poachers left the 200-pound-plus body to rot.

ANTLER CONFORMATION

Antler conformation is hereditary. In their management book, *Producing Quality Whitetails*, Murphy Ray and Al Brothers state that "not only is basic conformation hereditary, but oddities such as drop tines, forked brow tines, forked mainpoints, and roughness at the base are also hereditary. However, most of these characteristics are not evident until the third or fourth set of antlers."

Until it reaches two years of age, the deer's body grows rapidly. After that, growth is slow and normally stops altogether when the animal enters its fourth year. In bucks, most early growth goes into body weight rather than into antlers, which are small. But when a normal buck on good range is two and a half years old, more and more of its nutritional intake goes into antlers rather than into body mass. That is why each successive set of antlers is larger and larger until the buck is five and a half or six and a half years old and in its prime. If a deer

This splendid buck summered for several years near my home. The buck's right antler (left in photo) is typical in conformation. The other antler is not.

lives longer than that, the size of the antlers will gradually diminish with each passing year.

Keep in mind that whatever the conformation when the deer is three and a half years old, that same (or very similar) conformation will persist, only increasing in size, in future years. Thanks to this, it is possible to identify an individual animal year after year by its antler characteristics alone.

There are three basic conformation types among whitetails, all shown in the accompanying illustrations: "wide horn," "high horn," and "basket" horn. There are also nontypical (malformed) antlers, some so strange and massive that they defy description. The latter are caused mainly by screw worm infestations and possibly other debated causes during antler growth. The most massive deer racks are those that are nontypical, rather than typical. Some of these seem to explode crazily out of the deer's skull.

In fall 1981 a dead whitetail with this set of antlers was found in a field in St. Louis County, Missouri. According to Mike Helland, a state conservation agent, the deer would have weighed about 250 pounds on the hoof. But the nontypical antlers scored 325 7/8 points (Boone and Crockett), making it the most massive whitetail rack ever measured. This incredible set of antlers shattered the old world record of 286 points, which was taken in Texas in 1892 and which now hangs in the Lone Star Brewery in San Antonio.

Deer in different areas tend to have different antler conformations. This fine whitetail buck of LaSalle County, Texas, has "wide horn" antlers, common to that locale.

THE FUNCTION OF ANTLERS

But why do deer grow antlers at all? Of what use are they? Do bucks need them at all in a society that is matriarchal?

Particularly among whitetails, does are the dominant sex almost all year. And the older the does, the more aggressive and dominant they become. With rare exceptions, does feed first and longest on the best available forage, driving even their own fawns away if there is a scarcity. Consider another possibility: Large bucks spend most of their lives alone or in small bachelor groups, simply because the does drive them into this segregation. Even during autumn, when the bucks are carrying their fine polished antlers, does still

This whitetail in McMullen County, Texas, is a fine if not an exaggerated example of "high horn" antler conformation. The buck had higher and slightly heavier antlers the year before I shot this picture.

Huge body size does not guarantee heavy antler growth. This buck, photographed in the Alberta Rockies, has average or less than average antler growth relative to its body dimensions. Nutritional deficiency or genetics may be the cause.

retain the upper hand. I have often witnessed females reject the advances of, or even drive away, bucks much larger than they, until *they* are ready to be bred. Older females seem especially irritable.

So, again, what use are the deer's antlers?

One possibility, but only a theory, is that the size of a buck's antlers determine its place in the local hierarchy. The more impressive the rack, the more superior the deer and the more likely it is to breed the does coming into estrus. During the rut, deer do use their antlers to fight, and sometimes to fight viciously. The sharp points at times inflict serious injury. But size of antlers alone does not always determine the winner. Nor, in fact, do the heaviest bucks always have the heaviest antlers. Far, far from it. But there is some support for the theory that antlers help establish dominance among males during the rut.

Another common theory is that deer grow antlers to defend against natural enemies. If so, then why don't does have them as well? In either case, bucks have hardened antlers that are useful for defense for only three months of the year. It appears that antlers would be good defensive weapons, but bucks under attack instead rely on their great speed and agility to escape. If that fails, they kick and slash with their sharp hoofs.

Several years ago, while bowhunting from a treestand in a Maryland woodlot, I had a ringside seat for a near tragedy. It was early morning and I could hear a pack of dogs chasing an animal (a raccoon or an opossum, I first thought) not far away. But soon the chase turned directly toward my stand and I saw an injured buck being pursued and attacked by a group of mongrel dogs. The buck had

a fine, high rack, but when the dogs closed in it held its head fairly high and lunged toward the dogs with forefeet alone. It managed to hold them off in that way until I climbed down from the stand and scattered the dogs, one of which even threatened me. Since that morning I have often pondered the terrible toll that free-running house dogs take on wild creatures year after year.

It seems that antlers are not really needed for defensive purposes. In addition, a buck has no antlers at all during the critical period—winter—when it is most vulnerable to predators.

From my own observations, mostly with Wyoming and Montana mule deer during the rut, antlers are not always the deciding factor in those

Photographed in central Manitoba, this buck has a good, but not trophy, size rack for a northern whitetail deer. Bucks in the southern part of the province have more impressive heads.

This eastern Montana whitetail buck, with a sleek, heavy, fully developed body, is another illustration that large deer do not always grow large antlers. A buck this size should have antlers two or three times larger than this one does.

head-to-head duels in which the antlers sometimes become locked. Most of the contests, with heads held low, are shoving matches in which balance is very important. Too often I have seen a younger, stronger buck—already on the scene with several does—drive away an older deer with larger antlers.

Another intriguing theory, suggested by Wisconsin outdoorsman Al Hofacker, is that large racks could be attractors. Maybe those splendid racks attract more does during the brief breeding season. The finest-looking bucks certainly appear to do most of the breeding. Since so much of this activity takes place at night, away from human eyes, that theory is only conjecture at this point.

Hofacker also notes that in regions with large deer populations, bucks may identify one another by their racks and thereby eliminate the need to test each other each time they meet. When in semi-captivity in large, fenced-in research areas, two bucks that have fought to the point where one has emerged the clear-cut winner will not bother to fight again until old age or illness changes the relationship of strength. It is therefore possible that once dominance is established, every wild buck will thereafter know its place in a herd or in a given locality by visual assessment.

Although we have no absolute reason as to why deer have antlers, we certainly know that some sport much more impressive and handsome racks than others. When we refer to a good or big old buck, we mean one with great antlers—with what hunters would call a trophy or a bragging-size rack.

This fat and healthy Montana mule deer has not yet developed the widespread rack common to the species.

The uneven growth of this whitetail buck's antlers is more likely an inherited trait than the result of early injury.

BOONE AND CROCKETT CLUB CATEGORIES

We also have a system of measuring or scoring native deer racks. Administered by the Boone and Crockett Club, the record-keeping system divides our deer into six categories and lists those in each division according to size.

The six categories include typical and nontypical heads of whitetail and mule deer, plus a single "typical" category each for blacktails and Coues' (pronounced *kews*) whitetails, a small subspecies of Arizona, New Mexico, and Mexico. Typical heads are those with symmetrical or almost symmetrical antlers, the beams and points being nearly the same on each side. Most bucks have typical heads. Nontypicals are those malformed

heads, with an asymmetrical arrangement or unequal number of points on each side, the antlers usually bizarre in shape. Just the same, some nontypical racks can be impressive.

Using the Boone and Crockett Club's measurement system, a deer's antlers are rated according to the length of the main beams, the length of all normal points, the greatest inside spread between right and left antlers, and the circumference of the main beams at several places. All these measurements are made in inches to the closest eighth of an inch. The total of all measurements is the prelimi-

No trophy buck, this whitetail still carries a handsome 10-point rack with a single drop point. This deer is five and a half to six and a half years old, and almost certainly has attained its maximum antler growth.

Here is another view of the five-and-a-half-year-old super whitetail shown at the beginning of this chapter. His antlers here would probably have scored high in the Boone and Crockett records and undoubtedly would have been even more impressive the following year if poachers had not intervened.

nary score. Deductions are made for asymmetry —that is, differences between the basic measurements of the right and left antlers.

In the typical categories, deductions are made for all abnormal points. A nontypical rack is scored in the same way, except that abnormal points are added to the score rather than subtracted from it.

But what exactly is a trophy deer? Antler sizes vary greatly from state to state, county to county, and even subspecies to subspecies. In addition, one man's standards differ greatly from another's. Byron Dalrymple, a well-known outdoor writer, feels that "any antler size is directly proportional to a person's adrenaline flow at the time he sees the deer."

To qualify as a trophy rack here, and this is strictly my own rating, a typical whitetail should score 150 Boone & Crockett points and a nontypical should be at least 180. For mule deer, make it 175 points typical and 195 nontypical. For blacktails, typical or nontypical, the minimum could be placed at 100 points.

To score 150, a typical whitetail buck would have to have 10 points, five per side, symmetrical in shape, with an inside spread of 20 inches or more, plus long, heavy beams that measure more than five inches in circumference near the head or base. Not every deer of this loose description will score 150 points, but it will come very close and many will exceed it.

For official score charts, record books, and further information, write Boone and Crockett Club, 205 South Patrick Street, Alexandria, VA 22314.

ESTIMATING TROPHIES ON THE HOOF

Now consider the complications if you go looking for a 150-point whitetail. No other horned or antlered species is as difficult to observe long enough to judge on the hoof as a whitetail. The only one as tough or tougher would be the blacktail. By contrast, it is often possible to evaluate the size of the horns of a bighorn ram or a billy goat or the antlers of a caribou from every angle for a long time through a spotting scope or a long telephoto lens. Even mule deer can sometimes be evaluated at long range. But few whitetails give a person a long look. Most vanish in an instant.

To get a better conception of trophy and near-trophy deer, study all those illustrated in this book, especially in this chapter. Then, to recognize a trophy rack in the field when you see it, keep a few figures in mind. A whitetail buck measures 15 to 18 inches from ear tip to ear tip if both ears are cocked naturally, slightly upward. The average healthy buck is about 15 inches thick through the body. If the antlers extend several inches beyond the ear tips or beyond the body on each side, you are looking at a fine specimen.

There are also a few other rules of thumb. After checking the spread, look at antler height, which is the length of the tines. On a trophy whitetail head, at least some points visible from the front should be as long or longer than the ears. Focus your attention on the antlers from directly in front of the deer for the best evaluation. Forget about body size and disregard any other deer nearby. Concentrate on the one. Count the points. You want to see 10 or more on that whitetail. Notice the thickness and color of the antlers; the heavier and darker, the better. No matter what your purpose,

evaluating deer heads in the field can be a fascinating and thrilling game—a genuine test of your outdoors ability.

I have made my share of mistakes in evaluating mule deer antlers in the wild. Too often the buck I photographed standing on a mountainside did not have as massive a rack on the color slide as when I first saw it (too briefly) through the camera's viewfinder. As with whitetails, a mule deer must be observed directly from the front, and from as many other angles as possible, to be judged with assurance. A truly large rack will either extend well beyond the ear tips, when the ears are in their normal erect position, or be at least 15 inches higher than the forehead, or both. A typical mule deer trophy would have a minimum of four points and probably six or more per side. All of the beams and tines would be noticeably thick. Often the difference in scoring between two bucks of similar size is that one of them has much heavier antlers.

According to current Boone and Crockett all-time records, super mule deer have come from New Mexico northward to British Columbia and all Rocky Mountain states in between. By far the greatest number originated in Colorado. On the other hand, trophy whitetail heads have not been so concentrated in any one area. Record-book entries come from everywhere in the eastern two-thirds of North America. The prairie provinces of Canada once produced the biggest whitetails, but there now seems to be a shift southward. Missouri has become a premier trophy state. Perhaps the largest whitetail bucks of the future will come from the Texas brush country, where ranchers use selective breeding programs designed to produce large antlers. The largest blacktail antlers tend to develop in Oregon.

For mass and estimated weight of the antlers, this Alberta buck is undoubtedly the largest mule deer I have ever seen. The lower main beams are nearly as heavy as a man's forearms. What is not readily apparent in the photos, unfortunately, is the buck's tremendous size.

CHAPTER 6
EXOTIC SPECIES

For better or worse—usually worse—exotic big game animals have been introduced into the North American continent without heed of possible consequences. Deer from other parts of the world, especially from Asia, are the species most commonly introduced. To date these exotic deer have been put mainly into whitetail areas, rather than into mule deer or blacktail areas.

When exotic deer are stocked in good whitetail habitat the result is predictable. The whitetails soon deteriorate, both in size and numbers, as the exotic populations increase. The decline is traceable to lower nutritional levels caused by greater competition for available food supplies. Most exotic deer can eat substantial amounts of grass as well as the brush and forbs that are primary foods in whitetail diets; whitetails cannot eat the grass, however. Many controlled experiments have proven that the introduced species soon win the survival competition with whitetails in almost any habitat.

Savvy deer biologists agree that exotics and whitetails (or mule deer, for that matter) should never be mixed in an area because, when the two are combined, neither can be managed effectively. The only justifiable stocking of exotics would be on ranges that are totally unsuitable for native deer, and then only when enclosed by a high fence.

Unfortunately a lot of exotics already roam the land, especially in Texas and the Southwest. The most recent estimate is that 80,000 exotic animals of 31 species live in Texas. The first U.S. territory

My candidate for the most handsome deer in the world is the chital, or spotted deer, a native of southern Asia. It may now be more abundant on Texas ranches than in the area of its origin. Unfortunately, the chital is a serious competitor of the whitetail deer, which rarely thrive when chital are introduced into the same habitat.

As attractive as they are, chital deer are capable of quickly destroying habitat when they are allowed to multiply unchecked. I have seen areas where the species has eaten vegetation down to bedrock, as beside this south Texas water tank.

importation may have occurred in 1867, when a shipment of chital, or axis deer, from India arrived in Hawaii as a gift to the king. The species thrived and still survives on Oahu, Molokai, and Lanai, but it has caused inestimable damage to native vegetation. During the past century, there have been many importations of exotic deer, many of them done surreptitiously and without authorization, so that no complete record exists. Fortunately, many re-leases failed and have been forgotten. But we have ample evidence that exotics can adapt and flourish.

At present, fallow, chital (axis), and sika deer live wild or semi-wild or at least unconfined on many ranches throughout Texas. Some of these ranches are seriously overpopulated with exotics despite year-around sport or trophy hunting. The range has suffered terribly. Fallow deer also live in the wild in Kentucky, California, and probably in Florida. Sambar deer are established on Saint Mark's National Wildlife Refuge on an island off the northwest coast of Florida. There are many other limited or confined populations of exotics scattered about, mostly on large estates, which in time could escape or be freed.

CHITAL (AXIS) DEER

The alien chital, or axis deer (*Axis axis*), has prospered more than any other exotic. Called chital (in India and Sri Lanka, where it originates), as well as axis and spotted deer, the chital is the most handsome of all deer. I have seen great herds of chital in Kanha National Park in central India, where they are the principal prey of tigers and leopards. But today, chital are probably more abundant in Texas than in India.

The pelage of the chital, at all ages and in all seasons, is rufous-fawn in color, interrupted with white spots. When full-grown, the chital is about the size of an average mule deer. The antlers grow to fairly impressive dimensions. In the United States the antlers may be in velvet or scraped bare for the rut at any time of year. I've often seen chital with both velvet and polished antlers in the same pasture. These aliens are prolific breeders, and fawns may be born at any time of year, usually two but occasionally even three at a time.

Chital are mostly deer of open country—of grasslands—rather than of woodlands. The chital are extremely striking in appearance, but they are not as fast afoot as whitetails. A normal set of antlers has six points, though I have seen several trophy-sized chital on a ranch near Austin, Texas, with eight points—and one deer with 10. Of the chital I saw in India, none were as large as their emigrant brothers.

Chital utter a shrill whistle when they are alarmed, which surprised me when I first heard it. Early one morning, in India, I was watching a bachelor herd walk single file along a low knoll overlooking a misty pond. Suddenly the first buck stopped and whistled in alarm. The sound was repeated all down the line. Each deer stood alert and studied the pond. Looking through binoculars, I saw a tiger emerge from tall, damp grass to drink. The deer remained nervous long after the tiger disappeared, in the opposite direction. Later I learned that during the rut chital bucks utter a whistle similar to the alarm, but longer and louder.

FALLOW DEER

Next to the chital, the fallow deer (*Dama dama*) is the most widespread exotic in America. Most fallow deer introduced to North America came from France and Britain. Biologists are uncertain whether fallow deer were native to northern Europe

Heavy palmated antlers are the most distinguishing features of fallow deer, which reached America from northern Europe. They are the common species of deer parks and of children's petting parks, but they can be very wary in the wild.

or whether they had been imported from the Mediterranean region. One race, the Persian fallow deer, may still survive on a small reserve in Iran, if the recent revolution didn't wipe them out.

Perhaps no other mammal living in the wild has more color variations than the fallow deer. The so-called "typical" fallow is fawn-colored with white spots in summer, and is uniformly gray-brown in winter. In Europe, there is also an all-white fallow and a solid black or melanistic deer. In addition to these three, there are cream, and even silver-blue coats that have resulted from selective breeding in European game parks for many centuries. But on Texas ranches, I've seen only the "typical" pelage.

A mature fallow buck that has enjoyed good nutrition on an open range is an impressive animal with an impressive rack. The conformation of its antlers falls somewhere between that of a mule deer and a moose. Typical antlers are palmated at the top with brow and tray tines. Some game managers believe that the palmated fallow antlers take longer to reach their full mass than those of other deer of equal body size.

The rut takes place in late October and November. Then the largest bucks tend to be very vocal. Their deep rolling grunts carry for long distances. Following these sounds, I have been able to find the bucks without difficulty.

Although fallow deer are generally associated with peaceful deer parks and petting parks for children, the species becomes furtive and suspicious in the wild. More than once, the large bucks have eluded my camera, even during the rut, when most bucks tend to be less cautious.

Fallow deer come in more color variations than any other mammal species. This black-phase fallow deer was filmed on a farm in Washington state.

India and southeastern Asia are the ancestral homes of the sambar deer, which is a somewhat aquatic species. It now exists in the wild in Florida, and its range could begin to extend elsewhere in the swampy Southeast. I photographed this buck in Sri Lanka, near India.

SAMBAR

Sambar (*Cervus unicolor*) are about the size of our Rocky Mountain elk and are in fact closely related to them. The number of sambar roaming free in North America is still small. However, suitable swamp-woodland habitat exists all across the South, so the range of the sambar could expand. The sambar is a uniformly brown deer with coarse hair. In India, Sri Lanka, and southeastern Asia, where I have photographed them in the wild, old males tend to be much darker than females or immature males. They are never far from water, and they are often in it.

Even the largest sambar antlers are unimpressive when compared to other deer, be they native or exotic. The antlers consist of a terminal, forward-facing fork and two brow tines that protrude from the main beam at an acute angle. Bucks select a territory during the rut and spend a lot of time bellowing there. Apparently bucks do not try to assemble a harem, but the does do seem attracted by the bellowing.

The stocks of sika deer in the United
States and Canada are of different
races from different parts of Asia.
Those living on several Texas ranches
are consequently a composite species.

SIKA DEER

At least 13 subspecies of sika deer (*Cervus nippon*) inhabit the Far East from Viet Nam to Manchuria and from Tibet to Japan. Most are about the size of small whitetails, and the sika deer is now well-established in a number of North American locales. It is impossible to say which race, or which mixture of the 13 races, is the source of the North American stock. These deer are generally dark and drab in color. Here the bucks don't grow large antlers, but on Hokkaido, Japan, antler main beams have measured at 29 inches.

If its present foothold in America were to be somehow extended, the sika deer could become a serious threat to northern whitetails and perhaps to

mination, as two sika bucks did on a Manitoba game farm. Whether fighting in the wild is just as vicious, I cannot say.

In 1971 Texas researchers began an experiment to determine the implications of stocking sika deer in the wild, and also of the sika's impact on native whitetail deer. Researchers released two sika bucks and four sika does in a 96-acre escape-proof pasture on the Kerr Wildlife Management Area. They also placed two whitetail bucks and four whitetail does inside the same area.

The plan was to avoid disturbing the deer in any manner. There were no predators inside the fence, and there would be no hunting. The alien deer were able to mingle freely with the whitetails.

The sika deer, here bellowing during the rut in northern Alberta, is another widely distributed Asian species. It has the capability of living in the harsh climate of northern North America, if it were ever released there.

mule and blacktail populations as well. For one thing, sikas are forest deer (as are whitetails), and it is well-established that they can easily survive Michigan winters. They can also eat a greater variety of plants than whitetails. There is obviously potential danger here.

I have seen bucks of all our native deer species in combat during the fall rut, but I have never seen two bucks fight as savagely, and with such deter-

No supplemental or artificial feeding of any kind was ever done. During the following three years the six whitetails increased to 15. The sika herd numbered 16. In other words, 12 deer had become 31.

Very little rain fell all through 1975, the beginning of a severe drought. By late 1976 only six whitetails had survived the drought, while the sikas had actually prospered and doubled their population to 32! Eight years after the experiment began,

Only a few hundred barasingas, or swamp deer, survive in one national park in their native India, where this picture was made. But small numbers live on Texas ranches.

A few red deer, closely related to North American wapiti (elk) and native to a vast area of northern Eurasia, have been introduced into a number of private lands in Texas. They have integrated with elk wherever both live.

late in 1979, the biologists counted only three white-tails and 62 sikas. A few months later in early 1980, the last three natives died. The experiment clearly reveals the folly of introducing exotic deer into the American environment.

The four exotic deer I've described in this chapter are doubtless on the American scene to stay. Other species exist here in various degrees of confinement. It is interesting to see them, especially the chital, or spotted deer, which are striking, elegant animals in any setting. But the truth is that the transplanting of almost any kind of wildlife to a new environment plays a very dangerous game with native wildlife. History has taught us that transplanting seldom works out well in the long run.

The red stag, here photographed on South Island, New Zealand, brought tragic consequences. An alien from Europe, the red deer multiplied so rapidly in New Zealand that it destroyed whole environments. The government then mounted a great and costly project to reduce the population of these and other exotic deer. This should be a lesson to us all.

CHAPTER 7
OTHER
WILDLIFE

Elk and mule deer occupy the same general range in mountain areas of the West. I have seen both fairly close together, but believe mule bucks prefer higher country in summer. Elk are stronger survivors in winter, in some measure because they can better digest the hay or hay pellets that people put out on winter feeding grounds.

Except in the Pacific Northwest, few outdoorsmen know the boomer, or mountain beaver, a small rodent whose eating habits have a great impact on blacktail deer habitat. Largely nocturnal, boomers are seldom seen and—despite the name—almost never heard.

Throughout the foothills and slopes of the north Pacific coast, from northern California to British Columbia, lives a tailless, reddish-brown nocturnal rodent commonly called "boomer." Some people also call it "mountain beaver." Both are misnomers because this rodent animal, which is about the size of a muskrat, is neither a boomer nor a beaver. It makes almost no noise at all except when its teeth crunch to chew vegetation.

The boomer currently plays a critical role in its environment. In the past, boomers simply ate the plants and saplings where they lived and their numbers were kept in check by mink and weasels, their primary natural enemies. In fact, mountain beavers may well have played a role in maintaining openings in climax forests where blacktail deer could find browse.

In recent times, however, vast areas of the Northwest have been clear-cut and reforested, and boomers have become unpopular among foresters and tree farmers because of their fondness for second-growth fir seedlings. The U.S. Department of Agriculture and other research groups have invested heavily in devising ways to eradicate boomers in newly planted areas. The success or failure of eradication efforts is very important to deer.

Boomers are only one of countless wild creatures that share deer country and which are part of the deer's ecosystem. Some have great effect on the health and abundance of deer. Some prey on deer. Others simply thrive in deer habitat. Whenever we search for deer we see these residents as well. They range from mosquitoes and deer liver flukes to boomers and bobwhite quail, mountain lions and Kodiak bears.

LIVER FLUKES

Let's say you are watching a whitetail doe feeding around the edge of a weedy pond in the northern Midwest. It is summer and the doe wades into the water and browses on aquatic plants. The odds are one in three that the deer will at the same time ingest encysted larvae of the deer liver fluke attached to the vegetation. The larvae enter the deer's body, lay eggs in the deer's liver, and reenter

The cougar (or mountain lion, puma, or catamount) once coexisted with all native deer, coast to coast. But the cougar has been eliminated everywhere except in scattered wildernesses of the West. There also are a few survivors in Florida's Big Cypress Swamp. Once considered a vermin to be killed by any means, the cougar is now recognized as a valuable predator that helps assure survival of the fittest deer.

A deer's biosphere also includes the tiny forms of life it ingests with water and plants. Liver flukes are borne into a deer's system on aquatic plants.

the water in the droppings, completing their life cycle. Fortunately, this parasite does not greatly affect the health of adult deer because any damage is slight. But in Wisconsin as many as 31 percent of whitetails examined at one checking station had been infected. And one sampling in Texas found a 69 percent rate. The livers of deer as far west as Oregon contained the same flukes.

COUGARS

Many animals have a much more visible and, we may suppose, greater impact on deer than liver flukes. During a summer pack trip in the San Juan Wilderness of Colorado, we once came upon a small mule deer buck that had been killed and partially eaten by a cougar only a short time before. It is entirely possible that our approach drove the cougar away.

"Damn cats," our outfitter muttered. "Before long they will have killed all our deer."

That wasn't likely to happen, and of course it didn't. The mule deer of that area are numerous to this day and the bucks grow to much better than average size. In fact, some of the largest mule deer antlers of all are produced here. At the same time, that particular area also still hosts a good population of mountain lions.

Several times during recent winters, we have spent time on a remote Trans Pecos, Texas, ranch that borders the Rio Grande River for some distance. It is a dry, spiny area slashed by deep canyons where few people venture. By looking carefully, it is never difficult to find fresh cougar tracks in the dust, or most often at the base of cliffs overlooking the river. We found one high cave where a cougar mother had raised a litter of kits. Just the same, that ranch was also the home of healthy herds of both mule and whitetail deer, as well as javelinas and turkeys.

Bull elk fight for mating rights in
autumn. In winter after elk and deer
have lost their antlers, the elk's superior
size and strength let it win the battle
for scarce food over deer.

Maurice Hornocker of Moscow, Idaho, knows
more about cougar than almost anyone else, having
followed and virtually lived on the trail of the cats
for a number of years, all year long. Using hound
dogs, he live-captured, tagged, and radio-collared
many of the tawny native cats. That way he was
able to track the cougars and learn about their
relationships with other animals, especially elk and
mule deer in the Idaho Wilderness Area. His conclusion was that, if anything, cougars have a beneficial effect on the mule deer herds that share the
range. Cougars are mostly opportunists and prey on
deer that are easiest to stalk and kill—the oldest or
youngest, the sick and the injured. The strongest,
healthiest deer are better able to elude the predators
and live to do the breeding. Survival of the fittest!

COYOTES

One of the most controversial of American
animals is the coyote, once a western species that

Gray or timber wolves are controversial wherever they live, and their role as destroyers of deer and other big game is often debated with acrimony. Wolves do kill deer, and in some places deer are the main prey species. But this predation is a beneficial role for the survival of both. Certainly there is no danger that any deer herds will be wiped out by wolves. The wolf in the photo is feeding on a deer that may have been a victim of winter starvation.

The controversy over the golden eagle's role as a predator of deer and domestic sheep is well-known. Eagles have been poisoned, trapped, and shot in so-called retaliation. Although the magnificent birds surely do exact a small toll of fawns, they are not population-threatening predators. The fawn most likely to be captured is the unwary or weak one. Wiser, fitter fawns will grow up to reproduce.

This coyote is one of four that had been feeding for more than a week on the carcass of an elk killed by a truck. The coyote is an adaptable and resourceful predator that is no threat to America's deer herds.

has gradually increased its range to deer lands of the East. In many parts of the country landowners are extremely paranoid about coyotes, which they blame for being even more destructive of sheep than of deer. Coyotes will certainly kill sheep and deer when they can, but I have to regard most claims of coyotes killing deer as suspect.

Time and again I have watched coyotes—one coyote hunting alone, as well as four or five together—trying to catch mule deer. But I have never seen them succeed, not even in catching very young mule deer, which can still run a lot faster than coyotes. Any coyote's best chance for venison must come very early in the summer when, by hunting relentlessly in an area where fawns are dropped, it finds a fawn that is too young to escape. The law of aver-

ages would guarantee some success for such a predator.

Another period of predation would come during terrible winters when the snowfall is heavy and deer movements are limited. During these times coyotes might make inroads in local deer numbers. But again, in the past I have joined state game wardens in checking out reports of winterkills by coyotes. More often than not we discovered that free-roaming house dogs from nearby towns were the culprits.

PORCUPINES AND BEAVERS

Because they are able to alter terrain to a surprising extent, some rodents, other than boomers described earlier, can have a noticeable impact on both deer populations and deer movement.

Porcupines, for example, can alter the composition of a woods by gnawing the bark (and eventually girdling) certain kinds of trees in a forest. Curiously enough, this selective killing of trees can be an aid to deer because it can create openings in a woodland which sunlight can reach. Browse plants for deer will then grow.

I was watching a muley doe with a fawn from a long distance when I first noticed this pronghorn buck tearing up turf with its horns, apparently to establish its territory. When it bedded down, still draped with prairie grass, I moved in closer and made this photograph. Pronghorn often share range, especially winter range, with western deer.

Porcupines can have considerable impact on deer range wherever the two coexist. Toothmarks are a definite sign of porcupine activity. The quilled animals are able to girdle bark, as shown, from large trees, and consequently affect the composition of a forest, though often favorably for deer.

A beaver's tree felling and dam building seem to cause duress for only one mammal: man.

Beavers often have an important role, too. Not far from our home is a mountain meadow bisected by a clear, cold brook. Late on summer afternoons when we went there to catch trout for dinner, we often watched mule deer does and fawns emerging from quaking aspen groves at the meadow edges. Later a family of beavers homesteaded the place and within a few months had flooded the meadow that lay behind their dam. Most of the aspen were felled. We never did see deer in that place again, but it became a haven for moose and waterfowl.

Beavers have greatly altered the landscape of North America, creating, destroying (by flooding), or simply changing deer habitat. Mule deer once grazed in the meadow which is now the beaver pond in the accompanying photo. The water is currently a magnet for moose.

MOOSE

Moose and mule deer often inhabit the same areas. Many times I have seen both on the same mountainside at the same time. Once, while trying to photograph a drumming ruffed grouse from a blind, I had both deer and moose stroll right up to where I was crouched behind a tripod. But mule deer and elk do not get along so well. Although they spend summers together in the same high country around timberline in Wyoming, conflict begins in wintering areas where snow may be deep and food scarce. Being larger, with longer legs, elk are able to dominate any winter feeding grounds—including (perhaps especially) those where food is supplied by humans. More than once I have seen cow elk turn suddenly on a mule deer that ventured too close to where the moose was feeding. The mule deer invariably turn away. Both mule and whitetail deer have a more difficult time surviving deep snows than do either elk or moose. The deer suffer even more when they must compete with elk and moose.

I have often seen the Shiras or Wyoming moose sharing the same range, in fact the same forest glade, with mule deer. The two do not even seem to notice one another. But the moose, with higher "reach," is a serious competitor for winter browse.

No American gamebird shares woodland deer habitat as much as the ruffled grouse. The bird explodes underfoot of the deer stalker every autumn. In spring, a wandering deer photographer is likely to find a male grouse, like this one, performing on a drumming log at about the same time fawns are being born.

In isolated sections of coastal Alaska, the Alaskan moose lives near or among blacktail deer. No great competition exists between the two members of the same family. These bull moose are fighting during the late-September rut.

RATTLESNAKES

During my decades as an outdoor photo-journalist, I have received a steady stream of interesting letters from readers describing their encounters with deer and the ways they've seen deer relate to other wildlife. Especially from the South, a surprising number of these letters have described incidents with rattlesnakes and how, by instinct, whitetails seem to realize the danger and give rattlers a wide berth.

A deer's responses to a snake may range from avoidance to aggression, but the effects of the two creatures on one another is only slight at best.

But one Georgia man, who was also a beekeeper, saw a doe behaving very abnormally one morning on the edge of a cypress swamp near his hives. The deer pranced and circled cautiously while intently studying a spot on the ground. Then suddenly the deer pounced and landed repeatedly on all four hoofs, not unlike a fox or coyote pouncing on a mouse. The performance lasted for a minute or so until the deer spotted the man and ran away. Checking the site of all the activity, the man found a large diamondback rattlesnake still alive, but badly punctured by the sharp hoofs of the doe. I have no good reason to offer why the deer behaved this way.

There have been enough authenticated reports of alligators capturing deer in the Everglades and Big Cypress Swamp of Florida, to consider the reptile a deer predator. But Florida biologists feel alligators have only a minor impact on deer populations.

BEAR

Many years ago another man wrote about a semi-tame whitetail doe that frequented the area of his log cabin in northern Wisconsin. In January and February he felled small trees as winter browse to sustain the doe. In fall the doe fed on red apples that fell to the ground in his small orchard. In summer she caused considerable damage to the man's vegetable garden, but he didn't care much. The sight of the graceful deer was plenty of compensation. That

It is doubtful that grizzly bears ever pursue mule deer, which dwell in the same high country in summer. But a bruin occasionally might capture a fawn or feed on a winter deer kill when emerging from hibernation. Any deer photographer in the Rockies is wise to avoid grizzlies—always dangerous.

This is a black bear with brown pelage. Before Europeans discovered America, the black bear's range coincided almost exactly with the ranges of all our native deer, from coast to coast. Black bears still survive in wilder parts of that range. Although black bears are far more wary of man than grizzlies are, deer watchers might encounter them.

was especially true one spring when he noticed that the doe was accompanied by a new fawn.

One morning while cooking breakfast, the man looked outside his window and noticed that "his" deer was behaving strangely, running around crazily as if injured. Then he saw the reason. A black bear had grabbed the fawn in its jaws and was carrying it away. It was gone before he could fetch his rifle. The writer had never before seen a bear, or any bear sign, within miles of his cabin.

Possibly some black bears have learned to hunt fawns during the period when they are still vulnerable. But more than likely this was an uncommon incident in which a wandering bruin simply came upon a fawn.

THE SENDEROS COMMUNITY

Some of my most fascinating moments studying deer have been at Senderos, in south Texas, at the ranch of my good friends Hefner and Babe Appling. The ranch is unique for a number of reasons. First, it is managed primarily to produce large—trophy—whitetail bucks for hunting. Ten thousand acres of typical dense brush (excellent whitetail habitat) is enclosed within a 10-foot high deer-proof fence so that the herd can be managed and censused. Here and there on the ranch, tower blinds have been erected for watching deer. Narrow strips, called senderos, have been cleared of heavy cover by brushhogs and these clearings radiate as spokes from the hub of a wheel, outward for 200 yards or so from the blind. This is an absolutely ideal situation for observing the extremely rich wildlife community which thrives on the ranch. In fact I have never seen so much native wildlife anywhere

While waiting for deer from a blind, I'm often treated to close-up views of birds such as these cactus wrens.

in America during a single morning as I have from a certain blind at Senderos.

The first creature a watcher may see is a great horned owl flying silently to a final roost to spend the daylight hours. Dark red pyrrhuloxias, first cousins of the cardinal, flit about the blind, and one of these birds perched for an instant on the window-sill near my elbow. Cactus wrens quarreled around an old grass nest in a prickly pear cactus below me. A coyote drifted ghostlike across a sendero, and I wondered if it had been an apparition. Then I looked in another direction and realized that three deer,

An elk may be a bonus sighting for western deer stalkers.

all bucks, were standing in the open and staring at my blind which was a familiar part of their land-scape. I focused on the deer because this was the onset of the rut.

But the deer barely looked up when a second coyote passed within a hundred feet of them. And that coyote didn't seem to notice the deer. In fact the deer seemed much more interested in the large scattered covey of scaled quail which came along to feed practically underhoof in passing. The birds

This javelina was a nuisance for me. It kept eating the bait I had placed near a blind to entice a whitetail buck into range. The buck never appeared. Deer country from Texas to Arizona often contains javelinas.

seemed much more nervous than the deer. The deer meandered closer and closer to my blind until I could see the rough burling at the bases of their antlers. Then suddenly they turned and drifted away. I wondered if they heard my boot scuffling on the floor of the blind, or if they caught my scent. But a minute later I was aware of the reason for the hasty departure. The same deer that paid no atten-tion to the coyote and to the covey of quail moved away quickly when a troop of javelinas approached.

That was standard behavior. More than once I have watched whitetails relinquish a choice feeding area to javelinas. On other ranches I have watched the much smaller peccaries drive deer from spots where corn or other grain has been placed.

During my long deer watching experience in Texas, I have noticed that whitetails are even more intimidated by the feral hogs that proliferate on too many ranches. In fact these feral hogs may have a far greater impact on deer numbers and deer health than most deer watchers realize.

To begin, feral hogs can be highly destructive of deer habitat. They compete directly with white-tails for many desirable deer foods. And there is growing evidence that feral hogs, wherever they exist in numbers, are serious predators of fawns. In many hog-infested areas where fawn survival is low, the culprits probably are feral hogs rather than coyotes and bobcats, which normally receive all the blame. There is evidence that the hogs search systematically for newborn fawns in springtime. The truth is that feral swine have no place in the outdoors, and wise landowners eliminate them.

ON THE LIGHTER SIDE

Some encounters we have seen between deer and other creatures have been on the humorous side. Once in Michigan I watched a red squirrel follow three does for a considerable distance through a second-growth white pine woods. By staying in tree crowns almost directly above them, the squirrel seemed to be harassing the whitetails and for no apparent reason. At least one of the does was suffi-

A cock blue grouse displaying on his breeding territory is an aggressive creature indeed. This one attempted to drive me, Peggy, and a mule deer from what he regarded as his personal turf.

ciently annoyed by the chattering and commotion overhead that it quickly left the scene. The other two followed more slowly. But I have never found a reasonable explanation for the squirrel's noisy antics.

A more recent incident is a lot easier to understand. Peggy and I were photographing a blue grouse near the summit of Signal Mountain in Grand Teton National Park. The handsome bird was strutting and displaying on its breeding territory one cool May morning just prior to the mating season. With its tail fanned and ruby throat patch bared, its chest puffed out far beyond normal, the cock was a most impressive bird. Every time we tried to move near enough for close-up pictures, the grouse would dart directly toward us and try to drive us away. So we moved back and sat down against a rock to watch the show from a distance. That's when we noticed a mule deer buck with small new antlers in the velvet coming into the scene.

As soon as the deer reached the edge of the strutting ground, the grouse turned and "charged" directly toward the intruder, practically flying in its face. Caught by surprise, the buck only turned and walked in another direction.

OTHER WILDLIFE

Many of my richest outdoor experiences have come from unexpected encounters with other creatures in a deer woods. It is possible to spend an entire lifetime in good cougar country and never see a cougar alive. But I have been extremely lucky and have seen three, every one of them while I was in the mountains searching for deer.

The first wild turkeys I ever saw, in the early 1930s, were from a deer stand in a longleaf pine tree on Blackbeard Island, Georgia. The birds materialized from dense palmetto cover and stood in view for a few moments, burnished bronze in the first beams of sunrise. I have seen many turkeys

The wild turkey is another creature found in much deer country. The two are often hunted at the same time in the same locales. I have also photographed both from one blind. Turkeys add much color to any deer woods.

Locally, bobcats might be predators of fawns in the spring. They probably also prey on larger, weakened deer concentrated by snow in winter yards. But overall they are not an important factor, and now have become very rare. I have often seen bobcats while watching from deer blinds in Texas. I photographed this one in Georgia.

since that day, but none so dramatically or so indelibly branded on my memory.

The first bobcat I ever saw in the wild passed my deer blind. I was surprised at how quietly it could walk over a hardwood forest floor that was littered with crisp, late autumn leaves. A few moments later a whitetail doe came along the same faint trail. The deer was noisier than the bobcat.

Another interesting, perhaps seldom realized point, is that deer benefit from warnings of other creatures. The warning whistle of a groundhog in

No doubt the yellow-bellied marmot (the one in the photo is a black phase) has whistled many warnings that a human was approaching and so alerted deer. I filmed this one when I couldn't find any deer—a dilemma maybe attributable to marmot whistles. The busy rodents are pleasant to watch anyway.

Especially in the Southeast, good whitetail deer thickets are also inhabited by bobwhite quail. In fact, abandoned or neglected farmlands today furnish some habitat for both.

an eastern alfalfa field, or of a yellow-bellied marmot in a Rocky Mountain rock slide, could warn deer of danger. The same is true of a suddenly flushing grouse or bobwhite quail, or of a family of javelinas running full-speed.

If you go out in the field in a single-minded search for deer, despite your best intentions you will be distracted by other creatures. Once before

The morning deer watcher who climbs
to a tree blind before dawn and the
late-afternoon watcher who waits until
dark to descend may find their comings
and goings in a given tree coincide
with those of the great horned owl.

Anyone who wanders in northern deer country will eventually flush a snowshoe hare from the dense ground cover. The hare is likely only a minor competitor of deer for certain foods.

dawn, I climbed into a blind built low in a great old oak tree. As I sat quietly waiting for day to break and a whitetail buck to appear, I was suddenly aware of movement and what sounded like the rustling of wings nearby. A few moments later in better light, I found that I was sharing the tree with a great horned owl.

So the world of the deer seeker is never dull or empty. More species than I could mention here, and far more than I have seen, share the world of our native North American deer species. That makes our deer all the more exciting.

Far too often I have been diverted from the main purpose of a hike by stopping too long to watch and film a pika—always an appealing creature.

Moose standing seven to eight feet at the shoulder drive deer away from scarce winter food. Their great height also allows them to browse higher than deer.

Peggy and I have found blacktail deer and mountain goats living on the same ridges of the Olympic Range in Washington. Similar cohabiting may exist elsewhere, especially in British Columbia.

CHAPTER 8
CONSERVATION
AND THE FUTURE

A baited wooden box trap such as this is another deer-management tool. Although not an efficient or economical way to live-trap many deer, it provides a handy means to capture a few for examination or relocation.

Late in 1906, President Theodore Roosevelt created the Grand Canyon National Preserve and thereby made a terrible mistake. The preserve protected what was probably the finest deer herd in America, then or ever. About 3000 mule deer—all magnificent animals, outstanding for their good health, great size, and massive antlers—lived there on the one-million-acre Kaibab Plateau just north of the Colorado River. The herd had evolved in near genetic isolation in a botanist's paradise of pine, fir, aspen, and wildflowers. At that time, because bison,

An instant before, not a deer was in
sight on this Wyoming mountainside.
Then suddenly six does, hidden completely in high grass, stood up and we
had this family portrait. Though
beautiful in numbers, if the deer over-
populate their range, they can destroy
it and thereby themselves.

Sound deer management takes on many forms. This fine whitetail buck was flushed by the approach of a helicopter. A biologist in the helicopter was taking a deer census. By knowing the approximate number of deer in a given area, managers can better decide if the animals should be harvested or protected. (Photo by Murphy Ray)

This photo, taken in the 1920s on the Kaibab Plateau in the Grand Canyon, shows an overbrowsed juniper. Such overbrowsing resulted from man's elimination of deer predators and led to mass starvation of deer and to soil erosion. (U.S. Forest Service photo)

pronghorn, and other species were almost gone, the nation's mood had changed, and people wanted to save wildlife. Roosevelt's decision was generally popular.

But just before 1906, 200,000 domestic sheep, plus cattle and horses, had been released to pasture in the Kaibab. By the time the preserve was established, the livestock had begun eliminating most of the valuable perennial grasses. At the same time, a war on predators was declared to "save the deer." During the next 25 years, government-employed hunters operated on the Kaibab with poison, traps, snares, and guns. Their official scorecard of kills reads 4889 coyotes, 781 mountain lions, 554 bobcats, and 20 wolves. This total does not include the additional number of predators destroyed by the sheep and livestock people.

The program appeared to be working for a period. In just one decade the deer herd doubled in size, and in 12 years it quadrupled. The mule deer population in 1918 was estimated at 18,000. By 1925, competent estimates placed the figure at approximately 100,000—up from the original 3000!

At first glance, that may seem to be an extraordinary success story. In fact, it was a tragedy. George Shiras III, an eminent deer expert of the period, inspected the Kaibab and reported that the range had been practically destroyed and that half the deer were on the verge of starvation. What followed is a sickening story that must be told and retold so that people who care about deer will never forget it.

Initially, an attempt was made to trap the deer for transport and release elsewhere. But nobody wanted the few scrawny and sick deer that were found in the traps. Besides, there was no easy way to ship them elsewhere. Although it was apparent that immense numbers of deer would certainly have to be killed or somehow removed, the governor of Arizona resisted federal interference, just as many stubborn Western governors do today. During the next few years an insignificant number of deer were

Notice the plastic tag in this whitetail's ear. An immense amount of information about deer health, travel, reproduction, longevity, and habits has been learned through tagging.

removed by government hunters and by a series of open hunting seasons, when bucks only could be shot. Does were still protected. But that was like trying to check the spread of cancer with an aspirin. It was not until the 1950s that serious hunting of a herd suffering from disease and extreme malnutrition was finally permitted. By 1955, control measures had reduced the mule deer population to about 12,000 animals, the lowest in four decades of human error and wrangling.

The once splendid Kaibab has not recovered to this day, and it probably never will. A good many mule deer live there now, but the bucks are puny compared to the giants that lived there before the turn of the century. We have squandered a matchless wildlife resource, forever, in the Kaibab.

Two lessons can be learned from the Kaibab debacle. First, inviolate refuges for grazing and browsing animals such as deer will become death traps when predators are removed. The predator's natural role is to keep the plant-eaters in balance with their food supplies. Second, when the balances between plants and plant-eaters and between predators and prey are upset, man must function as the controlling agent if he wants healthy wildlife and a healthy range. This is the only way.

Fortunately, most of our professional wildlife managers and biologists have learned their lessons well. So have most informed outdoor people, hunters and nonhunters alike. But sadly, many politicians have not. Deer and other wildlife are still the frequent victims of ridiculous political biology, as I will show later in this chapter.

I don't wish to imply that the future of deer in America is bleak. Far from it. In fact, more whitetail deer—an estimated 12 to 15 million—exist in North America right now than when the continent was first settled. But we have not managed deer as well as we might have. Certainly, not all herds are as vigorous as they could be. Some states have too many whitetails for the deer's own good. Nor are mule deer in the West thriving as they might be if given more intelligent consideration. In fact, mule deer range is approaching disaster status in several Rocky Mountain areas.

Because so many of us are interested in the most widespread species, it is no coincidence that whitetails are the most studied of all our big game animals. Everything from the animal's life cycle to age structures and seasonal movements has been scrutinized. During the 1950s, the technique of live-capturing wildlife with tranquilizer guns was pioneered on Georgia whitetails. By this method, a dart filled with muscle-relaxing chemical is fired from a gun. When the dart enters tissue and the chemical enters the animal's bloodstream, the animal becomes immobilized long enough for a thorough examination and for marking. Marking is done in various ways, but most often by affixing a metal or plastic tag to one of the animal's ears, or by using a brightly colored plastic collar.

The ability to permanently mark deer has resulted in a tremendous reservoir of valuable information. From tag returns and recaptures we have learned much about deer movements—how far they travel, how long they live, and more. Radio telemetry—placing radio collars around the necks of deer—has recently proven especially helpful to researchers. For example, a biologist can now locate a specific collared deer at any given time. If the deer dies, the biologist can hurry to the spot and determine the causes. Through telemetry, deer managers are also discovering more about the effects of hunting.

MORTALITY

One important finding is that deer die of many causes besides hunting and old age. In many states it is possible that the annual hunting-season harvest accounts for less than half the annual mortality. In one eastern state the number of deer killed on highways annually exceeds 25,000.

There is also a high kill from another source

that some may not like to admit. The following true incident conveys the problem: Just after daybreak of a brutally cold winter morning, a conservation officer friend of mine answered his phone as we were having coffee together. On the other end an urgent voice said, "This is Joe. Our crew has been cutting timber over in Hansen's swamp. We've seen so many dog tracks that yesterday I hiked completely around the area to make a check. You won't believe

what I found unless you see it yourself. Can you meet me?"

We met Joe on the road to Hansen's camp, a cedar bog in northern Michigan that is about three miles square and split by a low hardwood ridge. The swamp has always been an important wintering area for whitetails, not too far from the outskirts of a small community. The more severe the winter, the more vital the swamp becomes as a refuge. We immediately found a maze of both deer and dog tracks, the heavier deer breaking through the crusted snow, the lighter dogs able to run on top. Within 100 yards we also found the first deer, gambrels cut and the throat torn open. Just beyond was a second deer, dead but uneaten. A little farther on lay a third.

There is no point in my describing the carnage in greater detail, except to report that altogether 24 deer had been killed over a period of a few days by man's best friends, running free. Outlaw dogs. All

Natural predators such as cougars and wolves take a toll on deer each year, but predator-prey numbers soon strike a balance that is healthy for all. Dogs, unnatural predators, often take a terrible toll on deer though, especially in winter when deer are yarded up near habitations in a weakened condition. Dogs learn to chase and kill for the joy of it and have been known to destroy many deer on a single outing—only to return home the gentle, affectionate pets that are good with kids and loved in the neighborhood. No friend of the deer lets his dog run in a deer woods.

were pets from a nearby community, where a leash law existed but was never enforced.

During the next few days my friend and fellow conservation officers put a stop to the killing by shooting several of the dogs. One was a collie-police dog cross that actually turned on the men when they found it dragging down a deer.

Many years later, living in Jackson Hole, Wyoming, I saw dogs from the town of Jackson running after mule deer that had been attracted to winter hay put out by well-meaning people. Al-

though the dogs soon gave up the chase this time, they did take a toll of these wintering mule deer, according to reports of the local wildlife officer. The number is, of course, impossible to estimate, but the winterkill of deer by dogs, nationwide, must be astronomical.

As I write this, a controversy is in progress over the wolves (and wolf predation on deer) in the Superior National Forest of northern Minnesota. Some citizens thereabouts are blaming wolves for all the ills that plague them, including the scarcity of deer. But David Mech, who has diligently studied wolves most of his life, made a startling discovery. He overlaid a map of deer summer ranges onto the same map showing the plots of wolf-pack territories. Most of the deer were found around the edges of the pack territories—in buffer strips or "demilitarized zones" where the contacts with wolves would be minimal.

Keep in mind that free-running dogs have no pack territories, or boundaries, to observe. In Concord, Massachusetts, two dogs drove a deer right through an open door and into the suburban home of Harold Boyle. Evading the dogs in a struggle that shattered the living room furniture, the deer escaped by crashing through a picture window. When last seen by housekeeper Christine Rose, the hounds were still in pursuit.

PRESERVATIONIST FOLLIES

Late in 1982, Illinois Congressman Sidney Yates opened a hearing in Washington, D.C., to determine whether the Smithsonian Institution could hold a deer hunt on its research center lands near Front Royal, Virginia. A herd of about 1000 whitetails lives there inside a deerproof fence on 3150 acres, an intolerable density of one deer per three acres. That's about four or five times as many deer as the place could reasonably support. In addition, parasites from the whitetails were infecting four species of rare and endangered animals at the research center. The bottom line, naturally, was that most of the whitetails *had* to go by the best and fastest means possible.

Qualified deer biologists from Florida, New Mexico, and New Jersey testified that the only way to permanently solve the Smithsonian deer dilemma was to hold an annual, carefully regulated hunt by sportsmen. They explained that live-trapping and removal would be tremendously expensive, if possible at all. Despite this, Cleveland Amory and other antihunting leaders entered the picture and protested loudly—as they had several months earlier, when another hunt was proposed to relieve a similar situation in Florida. The result was that the Yates committee took no action whatsoever. In other words, no hunting was permitted. As I write this, the whitetails continue to proliferate and probably to starve, in numbers far beyond their best interests. Again, thanks to biopolitics, deer are the losers.

One of the most publicized deer incidents occurred in the Everglades in July 1982. A hunt was proposed to harvest deer in that part of southern Florida where water mismanagement (again poli-

tical) has been threatening to destroy the Everglades national treasure. Many deer had been stranded on isolated islands of high ground, surrounded by water that covered areas that are normally dry. Isolated here, the animals would certainly die slowly. The idea of the hunt was to utilize the deer meat rather than simply waste the deer by letting them starve.

Again enter Amory and one Jack Kassewitz, Jr., of a National Wildlife Rescue team, who claimed he could save the deer by live-trapping them. He pledged to live-capture 100 of the animals if the hunt was postponed, which it was.

For the record, Kassewitz managed to remove just 18—all fawns. And three months later only six

When antlers of fighting bucks become hopelessly interlocked, one or both of the bucks will perish unless humans intervene to separate them. Of these whitetails in northeastern Ohio, one was saved. The other was too weak to walk away after an antler had been sawed off.

of the 18 fawns had survived. These six were being hand-fed and had no ability ever to live in the wild again. Now Florida biologists had still more evidence to substantiate their theory that deer should not be relocated onto ranges or into habitat unfamiliar to them. Still, this evidence was a hollow victory for biologists—the people who know most about deer.

THE BIGGEST KILLER

In the long run, it is not the killing by hunting, by dogs, by cars, or even by the strange mentality of politicians and Cleveland Amory that is the greatest threat to our native deer. Instead it is habitat destruction, the mindless expansion and never-ending development of the American environment —the loss of wilderness and open space—which in the end will eliminate our deer. Eventually it may eliminate us as well.

From the standpoint of wildlife and natural-resource conservation, the country has never known a more hostile national administration than that of President Reagan. Almost daily his appointed Secretary of the Interior, James Watt, has made decisions that are detrimental to, if not a total assault on, modern wildlife conservation practices. Watt's record staggers enlightened people.

During the past two years, wild deer areas that were once considered secure have been opened to unregulated development. Other precious public lands have been sold, and an even larger chunk of the public domain is being readied for a national tag sale. Budgets for researching our environment have been cut to the bone and then some. Watt has laughed at wildlife researchers as being "chicken people trying to look busy out there while on the public payroll." We know now that acid rain, which the president calls a red herring, is killing more than fish. Among other things, it is withering the vegetation that whitetail deer in the Adirondack Mountains and elsewhere need to live.

Of course our native deer will survive long after the Reagan administration. But the damage to habitat and the general health of our deer herds should never be forgotten.

Deer die from many causes, the most important of which is man's relentless encroachment on their habitat.

Murry Burnham hoists a mounted whitetail doe he calls Dodo for transport to a clearing. Murry had previously sprinkled Dodo with doe-in-rut liquid lure.

CHAPTER 9
FINDING AND OBSERVING DEER

Murry Burnham here rattles antlers to simulate sparring bucks. During the rut, this technique works especially well when the ratio of bucks to does in the vicinity is high.

It was a few days before Christmas and still pitch dark outside when Murry Burnham and I left a steamy, all-night diner on the edge of Pleasanton, Texas, and drove southward deep into the rolling brush country. Our pickup headlights did not penetrate far through the predawn fog that smothered the land. No other cars were traveling at that hour.

Night lifted to a gray dawn, and Murry turned off the main road and idled the pickup before a closed cattle gate. I opened it and we entered a pasture of mesquite mixed with crisp, brown grass. Live oak skeletons were outlined here and there against the sky. A troop of javelinas raced across our path and vanished into the gloom. Eventually Murry parked the pickup in a dense thicket and we stepped out. The eastern sky was pale lemon now.

"We'll give it a whirl here," my friend whispered, slipping into a camouflage jacket.

From beneath a canvas sheet in the bed of the pickup, Murry dug out a set of large whitetail antlers and what at first appeared to be the carcass of a dead whitetail doe. But the carcass was really a mounted animal—a complete whitetail hide stretched not too expertly over a papier-mâché form. With both the "deer" and the antlers slung over his shoulders, Murry led the way across a brittle, brushy field to a clearing surrounded by heavier brush. I followed with a couple of cameras and I noticed many deer hoof prints and a large scrape in the clearing.

First Murry staked his decoy, which he called Dodo, out in the open. Next he sprinkled it with one of the commercial doe-in-rut scents available on sporting goods shelves. Then the two of us retreated about 25 yards and crouched in shadow against the base of a mesquite. A few minutes later Murry began rattling the antlers. Earlier he had explained to me that he greatly prefers a large set of antlers, from a trophy-size buck, because the sound carries much farther.

For a while we sat quietly, motionless, listening and studying the lonely scene around us. A cactus wren quarreled nearby. Mourning doves flew in and dusted themselves near the decoy. Then Murry rattled the antlers again. The sounds perfectly imitated those of two bucks fighting.

Murry rubbed and slashed the antlers together, then rattled them against brush, pausing before scraping the tines over the hard ground. Then, abruptly, Murry stopped the noise. At that moment my eye caught a flick of motion in brush about 100 yards away.

Suddenly, a buck with a fairly good rack came running toward Dodo. He did not pause or hesitate or prance or look around suspiciously. He continued running directly toward Dodo.

Not until the buck was about 20 feet from the fake female did he stop, seeming slightly puzzled for several seconds. I figured the buck might turn and run then, but instead he approached Dodo from behind. He sniffed, and turned slowly toward us, as if looking for the rattling source.

Teamwork can pay off. Murry Burn-ham rattles up a deer while Peggy Bauer shoots, using a 400mm telephoto lens. Notice her steady camera rest.

From the time that buck came into the open and into telephoto range, I began shooting pictures. Some of them show the fine, sleek animal staring directly at me in disbelief. Through my viewfinder I counted eight points on a high rack. I could clearly see the moisture on his nose and the highlights in his dark eyes. I kept shooting until the camera was empty and the buck realized something was amiss. Only then did he bolt away.

The decoy doe doused with scent was the brainstorm of Murry Burnham, who must surely be the best wildlife caller today. The incident illus-trates how a combination of ingenuity and know-ledge of deer can make deer watching much more productive and a lot more exciting. At other times and places, Murry assures me, whitetail bucks have been so completely fooled that they have actually tried to breed with Dodo. Murry has pictures to prove it. Certainly this technique will only work during the peak of the rut, when bucks are likely to be attracted to the sound of rattling antlers and the promise of love. The technique is most effective where there is a high buck-to-doe ratio that causes great competition among bucks.

The buck is real. The doe is fake—Murry Burnham's Dodo, a collab-oration with a taxidermist. The buck approached Dodo, sniffed her, and looked around for the rattling source.

Antler rattling is an excellent way to get the attention of whitetail bucks in the rut, not only in Texas (where the practice is most widely used) but in other whitetail country as well. My friend Hefner Appling is the expert rattler here.

I have found that rattling antlers works as well on mule deer bucks as it does on whitetails. It succeeds especially well in areas where larger bucks otherwise tend to be especially wary.

A lightweight, compact cassette player that fits into a large pocket or pack can be an immense help for calling many kinds of wildlife, including deer, coyotes, and geese. There are tapes of deer fighting (sounds of rattling antlers) as well as tapes that provide instructions on rattling. The player can be powered by small batteries or a car's cigarette lighter.

RATTLING BASICS

Rattling antlers is a fascinating outdoor art. It works on mule and blacktail deer as well as whitetails. Where bucks are numerous, any kind of careless crashing together of antlers might be effective. At other times a virtuoso performance might be required to tempt deer into full view.

I made my own set of rattling antlers from a better-than-average symmetrical, eight-point rack with long and heavy tines. The main beams are about one inch in diameter and are cut from the skull just below the burl. This affords a comfortable hand grip, although the antlers are a bit heavy. I sawed off the brow tines flush with the main beams and sanded the spots smooth to allow ease of grip and rattling. I tie the pair together with a length of thong so that I can sling the set around my neck or over a shoulder.

Successful rattlers have their own special techniques which probably work as well as or better than mine. Well hidden, or in a carefully constructed blind, I first crash the pair of antlers together hard, then rattle the tines to imitate two deer pushing and sparring. I pause and repeat this at intervals, sometimes also scraping the tines on hard ground or against trees. Not all bucks react the same way. Some come bounding directly toward the sound while others sneak in a few steps at a time, unnoticed, until almost in your lap. Either way, rattling is suspenseful and can make the adrenalin pump overtime. During the "high rut" some bucks might respond at any time of day, particularly on cold, overcast days. But usually, the hour or so after daybreak is the most productive.

OTHER CALLING

Rattling isn't the only means of calling deer, especially whitetails. Or at least a skillful caller can often enough coax a deer into betraying its own position. Starting from scratch, if you don't have much experience with deer, the best results usually come from using tapes such as those prepared by the Burnham Brothers of Marble Falls, Texas. You

Peggy places a speaker, connected to a cassette player, in a tree. While a deer tape is broadcast, she will watch from a stand some distance away. A curious deer is most likely to go toward the sound and not notice Peggy nearby.

I blow a plastic deer call. Although I have not yet had outstanding success with it, Murry Burnham (who made the call) frequently uses it to coax deer into a very good photographic range. The technique requires a good deal of practice and experimentation.

This whitetail also was coaxed into photography range by rattling with antlers that bucks had shed naturally in previous years. This buck is practically running in eagerness for action. It lingered no more than a second or two after realizing it had been duped.

Peggy shot this picture of a whitetail buck that Murry Burnham rattled up to the front of the blind. Completely puzzled, it stared in her direction. An instant later it fled.

can use either their portable 8-track caller with amplifier or a small, battery-powered cassette player. Tape players offer an advantage over rattling because they allow you to sit some distance away, downwind from the sound to watch what happens. Intent on the sound, a buck is likely to ignore your position. But for many callers, using a tape player is not as satisfying as blowing on a mouth call, as I describe below.

Whitetails are curious about a great variety of sounds, even to those made on a predator call that imitates a stricken jackrabbit or some other animal in distress. Bucks will occasionally respond to such shrill tones, but in my own experience, does are much more susceptible. Especially in springtime or early summer, does may come prancing right up to a caller. A doe with a young fawn hidden somewhere

Walking slowly, looking carefully, pausing often in good deer country, you may see many more deer than you suspected could be there. We almost hiked past this buck which had bedded in snow close to the trail.

is particularly apt to respond to a sound that simulates a fawn bleating.

Even unnatural sounds occasionally seem to attract deer, such as the opening and closing of a zipper on a jacket. Writer Tom Mamich has described how he used an "ordinary, breakable rat-tail comb" to tempt deer into venturing closer. While holding the comb lightly in one hand, rat-tail pointing downward, he claimed he could imitate the guttural sound bucks make during the rut by stroking the teeth briskly with his thumb.

There is much more to be learned about calling deer and other creatures than we know now. A man who hunted coyotes in New Mexico reported that deer were attracted by a tape of a screaming flicker (a yellowhammer woodpecker). Murry Burnham sells tapes with basic deer calling and antler rattling instructions on one side and the actual sounds for comparison on the other.

Mule deer also respond to rattling and, sometimes to rattling without antlers. At daybreak one morning I watched a pair of good bucks disappear into a dense but small aspen thicket. From my concealment on a steep slope just above them, I would be able to see them wherever and whenever they emerged. But time passed, a snow began to fall, and no deer appeared. They may have bedded down. Idly I broke off dead, brittle branches nearby, scraped them over the ground, and then rattled them against bare tree branches beside me.

It was as though I'd raised the starting gate at a horse race. Immediately the two bucks broke from cover and trotted straight in my direction. Even the metallic cling of my camera's motor drive did not alarm the pair, until a cold swirling wind sent my scent downhill. Then both bucks turned and ran out of sight. But my photos of those twin bucks are a genuine trophy, despite the snowflakes that melted on the lens glass.

Of course, scratching and slashing the brush like that is useless, except in late fall, and doesn't work that well all the time, even during the rut. But the ruse is worth mentally filing.

The rut lasts only a short time, and no kind of calling is always dependable. So anyone who seeks deer for any reason must develop other, more basic skills.

HOW TO SEE DEER IN THE WILD

In almost any deer range, there are far more deer than most observers are aware of. It is possible to look directly at deer in a natural setting and not see them unless they move. I suspect that a beginner in the woods does not spot many deer because he just does not know what to look for. Many magazine covers and outdoor calendar photos (many of which have been my own) show a huge buck standing in golden sunlight, perhaps even silhouetted against the sky. These pictures are immensely appealing and attractive. But unfortunately, any wild buck that made a habit of posing nobly, antlers glistening, wouldn't reach a ripe old age. Semi-tame deer and those accustomed to people in game refuges are an exception to this. But when looking for truly wild bucks, erase the magazine cover and calendar

While skiing along a forest trail, we almost passed this small muley buck. Before it stood, only the antlers and dark forehead were visible above the snow where it had bedded. We pushed on immediately after taking this photo.

photos from your mind. Instead, peer deep into good deer habitat, which is usually dim or only dappled by sunlight.

Deer generally move farthest and most often at dawn and dusk, particularly at daybreak. So concentrate on seeing deer then. Summer and snowy winter are the best seasons because a deer's color contrasts most with the background then. In summer the reddish coats stand out against bright green vegetation, especially in sunshine. Contrasts, of course, are muted in shade. By autumn, typically, red coats have become gray, which is difficult to separate from the multicolored background. Gray is even harder to distinguish in a slaty winter woods bare of foliage until a blanket of snow has fallen. Then that same gray coat is quite visible against the white background.

Finding deer in any cover anywhere anytime becomes easier the more time you spend

The muley buck was far more nervous of our presence here than was the doe he had been following. If not for that doe, perhaps coming into estrus, the buck would not have stuck around for photographs.

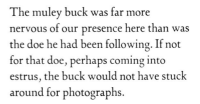

We heard this buck before we finally saw it, rattling its antlers in the dense tangle of alders. As we watched, it suddenly stopped rattling and bedded. We then moved in for this shot.

Cross-country skis or snowshoes are
the ticket for getting about during the
deep snow periods when any movement
is otherwise impossible. I greatly
prefer skis because they require less
energy and permit me to cover more
territory faster.

searching in deer country. If you sit on a stand or
walk as unobtrusively as possible through suitable
cover, watching and listening intently, a whole
world opens up. Then you will start to see deer and
other wildlife before you are seen.

Some of the best deer spotters I have known
were also year-round bird watchers and generally
enthusiastic naturalists. The explanation is simple.
Anyone who can quickly detect a white wing bar or
the tiny eye ring of a wood warbler in a tree crown

can more easily distinguish a deer's outline—or even
the nervous flick of an ear—in the densest foliage.
So it is good advice to practice bird watching wherever you live, even in your own backyard.

Avoid the mistake of looking to define a whole
deer in the woods. You rarely do. Small clues are
the giveaways. With experience your eye picks up
antler tips, head shapes, tails, different shades, tex-
tures, and lines which are not fixed parts of the
setting. It is not unusual for a motionless deer,
assuming itself well hidden, to allow a person to
walk past very near. But the more I have searched
for deer—photographing, watching, and hunting—
the more often I have found bedded animals playing
possum. Often only an eye or an ear betrayed the
deer.

EAR WATCHING

I am convinced that an observant person can
usually predict what a deer will do if, undetected,
he can watch the deer long enough. Or rather,
watch the ears, which are highly expressive.

Late on a golden afternoon in Glacier National
Park, I sat behind my camera on the edge of a forest
clearing where mule deer usually appeared before
dusk. The day had been warm and sunny, but in
the lengthening shadows I felt suddenly cold. I
slipped on a woolen sweater, gloves, and a knit cap
from my backpack. Five minutes later two doe mule
deer with fawns strolled into the open to feed.

A restless crosswind was blowing, and I'm not
certain if the four detected my presence. At intervals all would stare intently toward where I sat, and
all continued to browse nearer and nearer. Studying
the deer through the viewfinder and an 8-power
telephoto lens, I noticed an interesting detail my
naked eye missed. Although the deer looked mostly
in the direction they were meandering, all eight ears
were focused—aimed like small radar discs—toward
the rear most of the time. Eventually I saw the

reason. About 100 yards away and behind them, a fine buck, head held high, walked out into the last spotlight of sun.

Although the buck was a magnificent sight, the distance and the waning light prevented my photographing him. Ever since then, I have watched any deer's ears for clues to the situation and to help predict what might take place, all around. Often since then I have had advance warnings of hidden bucks and once of an approaching grizzly bear, well before it appeared in the viewfinder. Nine times in ten, a deer with "nervous" ears is ready to bolt.

DEER VISION

But keep in mind that any deer depends on all of its senses for its safety, although its vision may not be the best. (Many deer hunters will surely dispute my opinion that native deer have only fair vision.) Any deer certainly *can* spot the slight motion of a man in the woods, but that same animal may have trouble distinguishing a motionless and well-camouflaged person, even after staring at the figure for a long time.

TRAILS

Like any others who seriously search for deer, I am always, sometimes subconsciously, also looking for sign of their presence: trails, bedding areas, droppings, and browse sign. All of these reveal whether deer are using the area, and how recently. Trails are always the most interesting, perhaps the most important, and often the most confusing. Trails are also irresistible to follow, sometimes right to the deer itself.

Books on deer offer conflicting advice on the messages deer trails convey. "Sometimes deer trails are the result of years of travel," according to Ken Heuser in his fine book *The Whitetail Deer Guide*. "Other times the routes change suddenly, as if a

bridge were out. Don't take it for granted that last year's main trail is this year's main trail until you yourself examine it for recent travel." Heuser's theory corresponds with my experience.

A good time to scout for deer trails is just after a forest fire or a controlled burn, as done by forest managers. Any frequently used game paths are packed harder than the ground immediately surrounding, and the trails are much more distinct on bare earth in the wake of a fire. After a reconnaissance, remember where these trails are for the time when the vegetation grows back again, often thicker than before.

Of course the temporary loss of vegetation may force deer to feed and bed in other areas following the fire. But they almost always return and perhaps will reuse the old trails.

Aside from sightings of deer, deer droppings offer more clues to deer habits and whereabouts than any other sign. Ever since man has hunted deer, droppings have been a good indication of where to concentrate the pursuit.

According to biologist-researcher Rob Wegner, "deer droppings probably represent a better barometer of deer abundance and activity than any other sign." Although whitetails may eliminate body waste at any time of the day or night, the most defecation takes place soon after a deer rises from its bed. In other words the greatest concentrations of pellets tend to collect around bedding areas. If you find numerous pellet piles in one place, you have probably found a popular bedding site.

A serious deer watcher should be familiar with deer droppings, which vary considerably in size, color, and shape at different times of the year. A deer's diet also makes a difference. Very hard, elongated pellets are usually dropped in winter when deer are surviving on coarse browse. The later in the winter season, the harder and darker the pellets.

When summer comes, deer feed on softer, more succulent vegetation. Then droppings consist of clusters of pellets stuck loosely together. In some regions deer pellets could be mistaken for elk pellets. Summertime's fresh pellets are usually greenish, glossy, and very soft. The fresher the pellets, the more easily they mash underfoot.

It is helpful to be able to estimate the approximate age of deer droppings. The presence of many *fresh* pellets is, of course, a better indication of deer presence than an accumulation of old ones. Pellets will dry more quickly on the high and dry windy plains, where there is much sunshine, than in the shadows of a humid, lowland forest. Pellets dropped under dry conditions may survive intact for two years or more before they dry and finally disinte-

The elevated blind covered with burlap was in Maryland. The blind covered with tar paper was in Texas. Both required considerable effort and materials. But if such blinds are built to overlook popular deer trails, they give the deer watcher lots of action, especially if the area is also baited with grain.

grate. Where rainfall is heavy, the pellets may "dissolve" in a week or so. More than once I have been fooled by droppings, just following a rain, that appeared to be much fresher than they were.

It has often been stated, incorrectly, that deer size and even deer sex can be determined from pellet size. According to this theory, the larger the pellets, the heavier the deer and the greater the probability that the largest droppings were made by a buck. But this is merely myth. Researcher Arthur Smith of the University of Utah found that fawns often voided larger pellets than adults. So diet more than physical size or age of a deer determines pellet size.

Years ago in Beltrami County, northern Minnesota, I met a most dedicated deer hunter who used deer pellets for another reason beyond that of locating deer. During the hunting season he always carried a "scent box." Among the mysterious ingredients in the box were fresh, chocolate-colored deer pellets which he would scatter around his stand to help mask his own odor. He claimed that deer would often walk right up to him. Judging from the number of fine whitetail antlers nailed to his garage walls, the trick was immensely successful.

USING BLINDS

Deer are far better observed from blinds or stands overlooking busy, currently used trails, than by actually hiking or following those trails. In fact the best way of all to see deer, unalarmed and behaving naturally, is from a blind, preferably an elevated blind.

In good deer habitat, there are few dull moments when watching from a blind. Some of us are better, more patient blind-sitters than others. Some can endure the penetrating cold and the inactivity longer than others. But for a keen observer, usually *some* kind of wildlife is moving near any blind. Located beside a trail or where deer trails cross, a

As evidence that elevated blinds pay off, Peggy and I shot several magazine cover photos from this very blind.

This simple, portable seat can be fastened to a tree trunk at any height. Seated, rather than standing at such a perch, you will feel more comfortable and so will feel less need to move about and make noise.

blind may treat you to the sudden appearance of a deer, maybe just beneath the blind.

In the early 1960s, when whitetails were not as plentiful everywhere as they are now, I spent many hours in various blinds in Ohio, where I then lived. One of those stands was built in a giant sycamore where a well-worn trail crossed a narrow gravel riffle of an otherwise sluggish stream. The strip of dense brush provided almost the only cover in country that was mostly planted in corn and soybeans. This was not regarded a good deer area. But it was convenient to my home and easy to reach by an interstate highway. At times I could even hear the highway traffic from where I crouched.

During my first evening there in early autumn, I saw a red fox, several fox squirrels, a raccoon, and eight whitetails. Five of these were does, accompanied by three fawns. Next morning I counted seven antlerless deer, one of these passing so near I could have dropped a roll of film on its head. So the days went, does and fawns commuting between cornfields and daytime cover, sometimes pausing briefly to drink in the riffle. For a week, I saw no bucks.

One warm, still morning I sat staring from my sycamore perch into the empty understory all around. Green leaves were turning to yellow and brown. Nothing stirred. Maybe I dozed briefly. Then my eyes focused 150 yards away on the black nose and muzzle of a deer. The muzzle and nose became a fat buck still in the velvet, walking toward the stream and finally vanishing.

In the next ten minutes, two more bucks strolled by that spot. When I eventually climbed down from the blind, I found a second deer trail parallel to the one which passed my stand, but which tunneled—concealed—through thicker cover. Often since then, I have found that mature bucks do not always use what we might call the main trails, those preferred by does. Instead they may use nearby parallel trails. I have also found that it pays to study a wide area from any stand.

TYPES OF BLINDS

There are many types of blinds for deer watching, but elevated blinds are best. Usually, the higher, the better. The blind can be on the edge of a rimrock canyon in the West or high in a live oak in the South, simply because it puts you above the usual level of vision of deer. Many outdoors writers have stated that deer *never* look up, which is untrue. Deer do look up but only rarely or when they detect something unnatural.

Large trees with sloping trunks for easy climbing make perfect natural blinds. On some trees, it may be necessary to affix footholds or to clear away a few limbs to allow an open field of view. After the first climb, a rope ladder might help make later visits easier and safer. Be sure to have permission from the landowner before you saw, nail, or otherwise alter a fine old tree.

My most successful blinds have been those located and built for deer watching alone. I built them from scrap lumber, making them roomy and comfortable, with a good view all around. Your comfort in a stand is extremely important. Anyone can concentrate much better if he can sit down, uncramped, in a relaxed position. So my ideal blinds always had seats with room to stretch my legs, and with a section of old carpet on the floor to muffle sound. I always provided enough foot and hand holds to allow easy access in predawn darkness.

My comfortable blinds, though, have one immense disadvantage. I cannot move them quickly and easily to another site where all at once deer may be more abundant. Fortunately there is a myriad of portable and kit tree stands on the market, with a design to suit every possible situation. Many can be carried over the shoulders as backpacks. Advertisements in outdoors magazines should lead you to most of the options.

Still another type of blind which I recommend for very brushy or swampy whitetail country is the portable, metal tripod about twenty feet high with a 360-degree swivel seat on top. Even a household aluminum stepladder can give you some advantage in certain situations, though a ladder is cumbersome to carry. Or you might try a telephone booth-sized tent with zippered openings meant for bird watch-

ing. This tent by Eureka! makes an ideal deer blind and weighs only nine pounds.

But no matter whether the blind is only a sheet of camouflage cloth stretched between two trees or a permanent tower high above the ground, proper location is the key. Be sure your blind is placed where deer live most of the time, where they pass regularly, or both.

Light, portable tree blinds such as this are very useful for observing deer. They are not as comfortable as sturdier fixed blinds, but they can be backpacked to new places to follow deer movement patterns.

GETTING CLOSE TO MULE DEER

Blinds are not nearly as useful for watching and hunting mule deer as for whitetails. This owes to the habits of mule deer, which generally live in more wide-open country. But there is a technique nevertheless, for spotting and getting close to muleys.

Late in October in western Montana, I sat on a mountainside near the head of a vast watershed area. Several draws converged there just below lin-

For better or for worse, deer such as this muley are attracted to food handouts offered by well-meaning citizens. A photographer can take advantage of these feeding stations.

gering banks of snow. The melting snow ran slowly into the draws. I could see several other mountain slopes, mostly meadowlike, but punctuated with islands of dark evergreens. While scanning the landscape through binoculars, I spotted two mule deer bucks bedded down in the shade of one of the islands. They were extremely well hidden and perhaps impossible to see by anyone passing on the steep trail close by them. At this long range, one of the bucks appeared to have an outstanding rack.

This was the day before Montana's deer and elk season was to open in this region. As I watched, a packtrain of four men and eight horses approached on the trail from below, no doubt to pitch a hunting camp in the high country. Slowly, in single file, the men and animals neared the bedded bucks. I expected them to flush at any minute. But the train continued past and out of sight while the deer remained in their beds undetected. "They're a might cool," I thought to myself.

At noon I ate a sandwich and candy bar and

This cold midwinter scene may at first seem empty of deer. But look carefully at the bottom center of the picture, where a mule deer buck is silhouetted against the snow. I shot this picture from a car window, using the sill as a support.

was checking once more on the deer when suddenly both were on their feet and heading toward the rough cliff-and-rimrock country above them. Puzzled, I focused on the trail below—the same trail on which the packtrain had passed an hour before. This time I saw a solitary backpacker, probably also on his way to set up a spike hunting camp.

But the hiker was still 300 yards distant when the bucks spooked. Why? My conclusion is that a man on a horse can almost always approach far closer to mule deer than a man on foot. In the many years since that day, Peggy and I have horse-packed and backpacked countless miles through many areas of the northern Rocky Mountains, springtime through fall. Invariably we have seen more mule deer when riding than when walking. And we see them at much closer ranges. Incidentally, most mountain horses are excellent deer spotters. Watch their ears and watch where the horses are looking, and you will locate many more deer than with your own eyes alone.

Just spotting mule deer is a minor art itself. Far too often I have looked at ideal mule deer country with unaided eyes and seen nothing. Even checking through field glasses produced nothing—until I sat down and slowly, carefully glassed every square yard of the landscape. Only then did the forms of deer pop out at me from places I would have wagered held no deer. Through binoculars I once counted 21 mule deer on an avalanche slope where I had seen none with naked eyes. This was a lesson I have never forgotten.

I have no scientific data to support or refute one other theory, but my experience supports it strongly. Deer are far easier to observe just before a storm and then again just after it. I am not speaking of minor weather impulses which pass through an area, or of warm drizzles. But the more savage an approaching storm, the more active deer become and the less wary they seem to be. With a storm approaching, deer appear to feed in open areas, even at midday.

Later, during the peak of a storm, it is difficult to find deer. Almost surely they retreat to the heaviest cover. Then the next time to go afield is the first morning after a storm front has passed, leaving the skies clear. Take my word for it.

In Rocky Mountain mule deer country, it is often possible to approach closer to deer on horseback than on foot. You can also cover much more distance by riding. Many mountain horses are also excellent game spotters.

CHAPTER 10
PHOTOGRAPHING DEER

My wife Peggy and I have been fortunate to go hunting with cameras completely around the world. In our travels, we have focused on most of the world's big-game animals, from tigers and lions to polar bears and elephants. But few, if any, creatures have given us as much pleasure, nor have they been as challenging to photograph, as the deer of North America. In fact, our deer are much more difficult to photograph than some of the world's rarest and most endangered species.

One great advantage of camera hunting is that the hunting season is never closed. We can hunt whenever *we* want to go. There are no licenses to buy and no permits to be drawn. Any photographer can also go afield after big trophies. Once he has shot his prize, he need not stop hunting. Unlike the gun hunter, a photographer can keep searching for an even better prize. Indeed, hunting with a camera is extraordinary sport.

There are two quite different methods of hunting with a camera. The first and by far the more difficult is to proceed as a meat or trophy hunter would, going into open-hunting areas. This means investing much time and effort in a pursuit that promises small chance of smashing success. You must be a super woodsman or be especially lucky to shoot a gun-shy buck deer this way. To me it has been much tougher to shoot a photo of a trophy-size buck than it has been to obtain a buck with a firearm. The difficulty of taking a good, clear, focused picture of a trophy-size buck is about as

For Peggy and me, wildlife photography has been more than a profession. It's been a way of life. As you can see, we never smile.

There is no harm in photographing a fawn, such as this whitetail, in early summer. But after shooting a quick picture or two, you should depart. Resist any temptation to believe the fawn is an orphan that needs saving, because the mother is almost always close by.

This 35mm SLR equipment shot most of the photographs in this book. We depend most heavily on just two lenses, the Vivitar 70–210 zoom lens and the Nikkor 400mm telephoto.

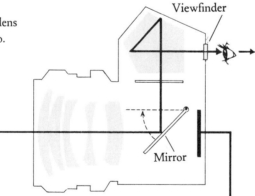

A 35 SLR (single-lens-reflex) camera employs one lens for viewing and exposing the film. Many other cameras manufactured today use two separate lenses for these functions. With a 35 SLR, exactly the same picture you see in the viewfinder is projected onto the film. The mirror reflects the image into the viewfinder while you compose your picture and then flips up out of the light path when you release the shutter to expose the film.

difficult as taking that buck with bow and arrow.

The second method is to photograph only in sanctuaries, parks, or other places where hunting is banned or where hunting pressure is light. Even in refuges our native deer may be shy, but they won't be nearly as wary as those on open-hunting lands. In refuges, a photographer almost always has a chance at a closer approach, and deer (he hopes) usually will not bolt the instant they see him. Many pictures in this book were shot in such areas.

BASIC SAVVY AND ATTITUDE

No matter where the hunting, a photographer's success depends greatly on his knowledge of deer. I hope earlier chapters are helpful in that regard. It is important to be able to distinguish good deer habitat from poor habitat, and to know if many deer are present in an area by looking for deer sign or lack of sign. Timing is also important. Early and late in the day, anywhere, any time of year, are the best periods, for photography and for deer activity.

The more time you spend trying to photograph deer, the better your results are likely to be. Eventually, a photographer develops a sixth sense or an alertness that tells him where deer will walk, when they will become alarmed, and what they will do after that. Success also depends on planning, plenty of determination, and patience galore.

It is possible to take great pictures by simply driving through good deer country soon after daybreak, maybe by shooting right from your car window. The average deer is far less afraid of an automobile than of a person on foot. But day in and day out, it takes more effort than that. For example, you need willing legs, spare time, and a little more photo equipment than the average photo hobbyist. Occasionally a supply of insect repellent is as vital as the camera.

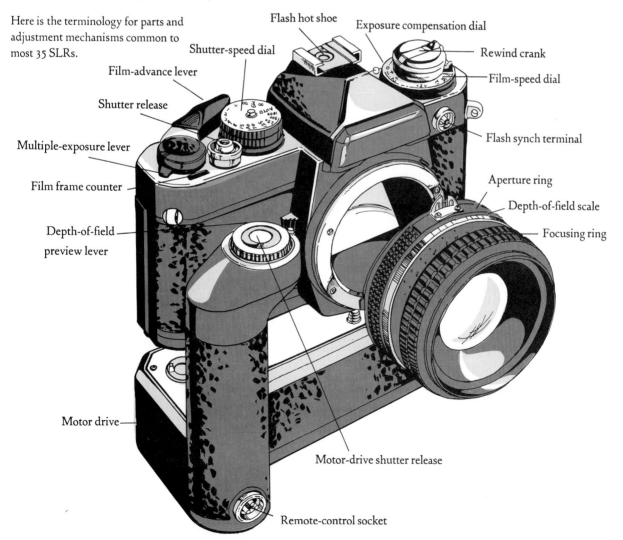

Here is the terminology for parts and adjustment mechanisms common to most 35 SLRs.

Flash hot shoe

Exposure compensation dial

Shutter-speed dial

Rewind crank

Film-advance lever

Film-speed dial

Shutter release

Multiple-exposure lever

Flash synch terminal

Film frame counter

Aperture ring

Depth-of-field scale

Depth-of-field preview lever

Focusing ring

Motor drive

Motor-drive shutter release

Remote-control socket

THE CAMERA

Exactly what kind of camera is best for shooting deer? Every conceivable type of camera, from pocket cameras to heavy studio cameras, has been used to photograph deer. For many years I used a Hasselblad $2\frac{1}{4}$ x $2\frac{1}{4}$-inch reflex camera for all my wildlife and other photography. The Hasselblad is a fine camera for many situations, but I no longer consider it suitable, or even adequate, for shooting elusive wildlife.

Any camera for outdoor or wildlife photography should be sturdy, reliable, fast to operate, not too heavy, not too bulky, and designed to withstand rough handling and abuse. It should function in extremely cold and very damp weather, as well as in great heat. Certainly it should feel comfortable in your hands. All things considered the ideal deer camera is the 35mm single-lens reflex, or 35 SLR, of which there is a bewildering number of brands and models on the market.

It would be difficult to select the *best* 35 SLR because today nearly all of the internationally available brands are technologically excellent. And some are nearly foolproof. These modern cameras make it possible for amateurs to achieve immediately what eluded the best professionals 20 years ago. And better models are being introduced every year.

A 35 SLR is a light-proof housing with five main parts. These are (1) the shutter, (2) the lens, (3) the film-holding or winding mechanism, (4) the viewing device, and (5) the exposure meter.

The shutter device permits a burst of light to pass through the diaphragm opening of the lens when the release button is tripped. On some of today's 35 SLRs, with shutter-preference feature, you simply set the shutter speed you desire (fast for action; slow if there is little motion) and the proper f/stop (lens opening) is automatically set by an impulse from the built-in exposure meter. On other 35 SLRs, with an aperture-preference feature,

For night photography and for flash fill in dimly lit conditions, there are cameras that automatically provide correct exposures when light from the flash attachment is reflected back from the subject onto the film, as shown. Or you can purchase flash attachments that automatically read correct exposures themselves and deliver light accordingly.

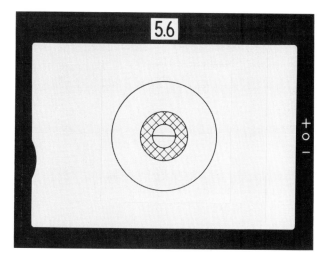

In the manual mode of operation, meaning the photographer has complete control of aperture setting and shutter speed, many SLR viewfinders show the aperture setting (in this case f/5.6) and indicate on right-hand side whether that f/number will result in a correct exposure—noted in this viewfinder by a dot that lights up between a plus sign (+), which would warn of an overexposure, and a minus sign (−), which would warn of an underexposure. (Drawings courtesy of Nikon.)

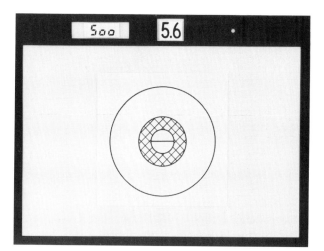

In the automatic mode, meaning the photographer sets either the aperture setting or the shutter speed, the camera's electronics automatically provides either the correct complementary shutter speed or aperture setting. The viewfinder here is that of an aperture-priority camera. This means you manually set the aperture for desired depth of field. Then the camera automatically selects the proper shutter speed, in this case showing "500," or 1/500 second.

you set the f/stop and the proper shutter speed is automatically set. Some 35 SLRs even focus automatically.

Most quality 35 SLRs also have shutter settings marked T and B to indicate Time and Bulb, but these have virtually no application when hunting deer. Shutters also have built-in synchronization for flash units. You might think flash capability would be of no value in big game photography, but on a number of occasions I have attached a flash unit to my camera to film deer at night or in very dark woods. The trouble is that you must be quite close to a deer to use flash. Even with the most powerful of today's portable, battery-powered flash units, a deer must be standing less than 40 feet away and usually much less than that. To ensure that the

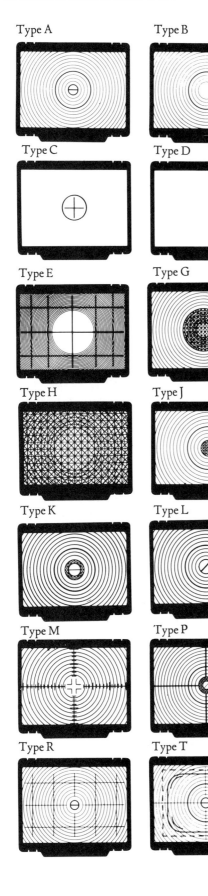

Type A Type B

Type C Type D

Type E Type G

Type H Type J

Type K Type L

Type M Type P

Type R Type T

Many different focusing screens are available for 35 SLR cameras. Those shown are offered by Nikon. But not all are suitable for wildlife photography. Which to choose is *a matter of preference*. Focusing screens are easy to change, usually by removing the finder as described in the camera manual. When changing a focusing screen, be careful not to touch the inner surfaces because this will leave fingerprints. Take special care to protect any screen from scratching or abrasion of any kind.

Type A is a matte Fresnel field with a split-image rangefinder spot. It provides most photographers with rapid, accurate focusing and is considered excellent for general photography. This type of screen comes with most cameras sold across the counter. *Type L* is similar to *Type A*, except that the split-image rangefinder line is at a 45-degree angle. This may be somewhat better than *Type A* for subjects with horizontal lines.

Type B has a matte Fresnel field with a fine-ground matte focusing spot in the center. It is good for general photography, especially for use with telephoto lenses. It is the screen I now use for wildlife.

Type C is meant mostly for photomicrography. The overall fine-ground matte field of *Type D* makes it a pretty good choice both for close-ups and for using a telephoto lens. This may often be the answer for the photographer who wears eyeglasses and who has problems using other types of screens. All of the other types shown here can be used for general outdoor photography but probably are not among the best for stalking deer in changing conditions.

flash unit is within range, you can connect the camera's shutter to a trip wire strung across a deer trail.

The viewer or viewfinder on top of the camera frames the picture you will obtain when you release the shutter. Here is where you actually compose your picture—where you see your deer or other subject—and adjust the focus. You hold the camera up to your face and place your eye against the viewer. This is a little more awkward if you wear eyeglasses.

On almost all modern 35 SLRs, the viewfinder is also a miniature instrument board where exposure information is flashed around the edges of the picture. In other words, while you compose and focus, you can take note of your shutter speed and lens opening without lowering the camera. The built-in exposure meter will also indicate, usually in color light or symbol $(+$ or $-)$ if your picture will be under-, over-, or properly exposed.

The film-holding and/or winding mechanism of a 35 SLR is a system of sprockets and rollers (with lugs to engage the notches along the edges of 35mm film strips) to move a roll of film, section by section, directly behind the lens through the pic-ture-taking process. The film is held flat when the shutter is released. A flip of the thumb on the film advance lever advances the film for the next exposure. Or the advance can be motor driven for smooth, rapid exposures. After the last exposure on a roll of 20 or 36 exposures, the film must be rewound and removed. Most film winders ensure against exposing the same frame of film a second time, which would otherwise cause a double exposure. This safeguard against double exposure is a boon when you become completely engrossed in focusing on a nervous animal. All film-winding mechanisms also include "windows" or counters to show how many pictures have been taken so you know how many more frames you have on that roll.

Most motor drives can easily be connected and disconnected from the camera in a few seconds. The newest motor drives (such as this MD-12 for the Nikon FM2) are lightweight and fit well in the hand. Using this drive unit, I have been able to shoot more than 100 36-exposure rolls of film with a single set of eight AA penlight batteries. This drive also lets me shoot up to 3.2 frames per second. But I rarely use the high-rate option.

LENS BASICS

The most important part of any camera is the lens. Your pictures are limited by its capabilities and general quality. The prices of most lenses reflect their quality. With an SLR, the lens "sees" the same subject you see in your viewfinder and then projects the subject onto your film.

Lenses are often described as being either slow or fast. Relative "speed" in this case means the ability of a lens to collect and transmit light rays. The speed of a lens is determined by the diameter of the lens in relation to its focal length (the distance from the lens to the film). For example, a lens that is one inch in diameter with a focal length of three inches would be an f/3 lens (or $3 \div 1 = 3$). If the lens were half an inch in diameter, with the same focal length, it would be an f/6 lens (or $3 \div \frac{1}{2} = 6$).

The maximum speed for all 35 SLR lenses is indicated with an "f" number—for example, f/2, f/3.5, or f/8. The lower the f/number, the faster the lens and the more light it can collect and deliver to the film. Here are some examples of relative lens speeds: an f/2 lens is four times as fast as an f/4 lens; the same f/2 lens is 16 times as fast as an f/8 lens. Thus, the f/2 lens is fast enough to take pictures under low-light conditions that slower lenses couldn't.

At one time, photographers had to wait for bright sunshine before they could shoot. Modern fast lenses make deer photography possible in any kind of light. Faster lenses also make it possible to use faster shutter speeds, and therefore allow you to shoot a deer bounding away without blurring.

Aside from differences in speed, lenses also

Focal length and lens speed are marked on lens fronts, as here. Usually, the lower the f/number on a lens by a given maker, the higher the price.

The diagonal of a 35mm film frame is 43mm, which is also approximately the focal length of a 35mm SLR's so-called normal (or 50mm) lens. The center of a 50mm lens is approximately 50mm from the film plane when the lens is focused on infinity. Thus, the longer the telephoto lens, the higher its *mm* number.

differ in their ability to transmit a sharp image to the film. Although speed can be stated numerically (as f/4), there is no sharpness indicator. Some lenses have it, some do not. In my experience, the more I've paid for a lens, the sharper it has been. However, almost all medium-priced lenses will be satisfactory for most amateurs. Only the professional or the scientist will absolutely need the very best and, usually, the most expensive lenses.

Lenses must be critically focused to obtain the clearest possible image. Focusing is a matter of moving the lens closer to or farther from the film. Ordinarily a lens barrel is fitted outside with a footage-scale or a zone-focus adjustment. These scales can be set to match the distance to the subject.

The selective focusing possible with a good

modern lens is wonderfully handy for outdoor photographers. With it, you can accentuate a deer by intentionally blurring and almost eliminating the background.

Although each lens has a certain light-gathering capacity, or rating, it is the diaphragm inside the 35 SLR lens that regulates *how much* of this light is permitted to reach the film. The diaphragm functions much like a valve in a pipeline: When the valve is wide open, 10 gallons of liquid per minute may pass through; the further the valve is closed, the less liquid gets through, and the longer it takes the same 10 gallons to pass. Similarly, the larger the diaphragm opening, the more light passes through the lens when the shutter opens and closes.

Diaphragm openings are known by various

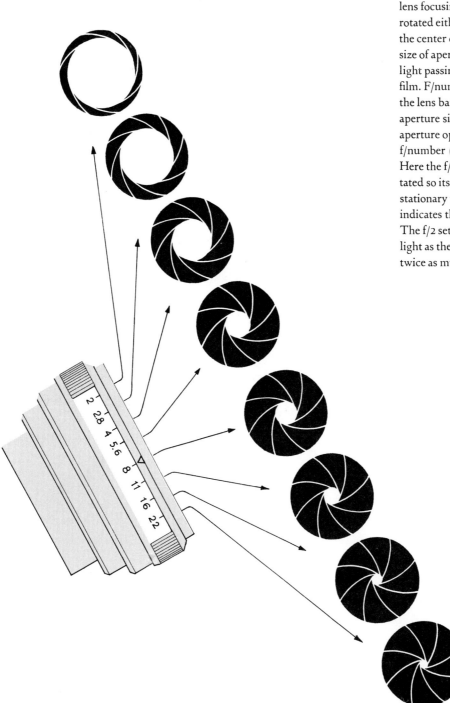

Inside every 35mm SLR lens is a mechanism called a diaphragm. This consists of thin leaves overlapped in concentric order. When you turn the lens focusing ring, these leaves are rotated either to open the aperture in the center or to close it down. This size of aperture controls the amount of light passing through the lens to the film. F/numbers (f/stops) on the top of the lens barrel, as shown, identify aperture sizes. This drawing compares aperture openings from the largest f/number (2) to the smallest (22). Here the f/number scale has been rotated so its number 8 aligns with the stationary triangle on the barrel and indicates that the aperture is set at f/8. The f/2 setting admits twice as much light as the f/2.8, and the f/2.8 admits twice as much light as the f/4, etc.

Different combinations of f/numbers and shutter speed allow the same amount of light to reach the film. To freeze a running deer, use the fast shutter and large f/number as on the right. To photograph a motionless deer and keep the background in relatively sharp focus, you might use one of the two combinations at the left.

names: lens opening, lens stop, f/opening, f/number, and f/stop. These diaphragm openings are marked with f/numbers—the same f/numbers I used in discussing the speeds of lenses.

For example, the f/2 lens on one of my cameras has diaphragm openings marked f/2, f/2.8, f/4, f/5.6, f/8, f/11, f/16, and f/22. The amount of light is regulated by changing from one of these f/stops to another, from maximum light at f/2 to minimum light at f/22. The intervals between these f/numbers on my lens, and most lenses, are called full stops because f/2 is twice as fast (admits twice as much light) as f/2.8, and f/8 admits twice as much light as f/11, and so on. On many cameras, it is possible to set the diaphragm opening at half stops—or halfway between the full stops—for more eaxct exposures.

This is a good place to briefly approach the matter of exposures. Since f/8 permits twice as much light to reach the film as f/11, a picture of a stationary object taken at f/8 with a shutter speed of 1/100 second will have the same exposure as if taken at f/11 and 1/50 second. This is because 1/50 second allows light to penetrate twice as long as 1/100, and it thereby compensates for f/11 passing only half as much light as f/8. In other words, you can halve or double the amount of light striking the film by altering the f/stop one full stop, down or up, or by halving or doubling the shutter speed.

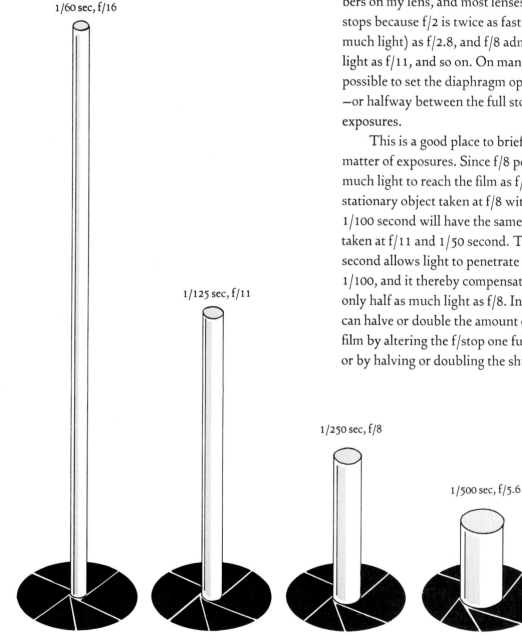

1/60 sec, f/16

1/125 sec, f/11

1/250 sec, f/8

1/500 sec, f/5.6

1/1000 sec, f/4

When using a long telephoto lens, as here with a 300mm, it is difficult to achieve much depth of focus (depth of field). In this photo, only the nearest buck is in focus. I might have brought the other deer into sharper focus with a slower shutter speed and a smaller lens opening, but in doing that, camera motion might have created blurring. In any case, when shooting two or more animals at different distances from the camera, it is best to keep the nearest and most prominent deer in sharpest focus.

Now look at it another way: f/11 at 1/50 second *equals* f/8 at 1/100 *equals* f/5.6 at 1/200 *equals* f/4 at 1/400, and so on. The total amount of light received by the film is the same whether it is a bright light for a short period of time, or a dim light for a long time. The principle is similar to filling a bucket with a large stream of water for a short time or with a thin stream of water for a much longer time.

Another function of the diaphragm, in conjunction with the lens, is to control depth of field. This is the distance in front of and behind the subject within which all objects are in focus. The *larger* the f/number (which means, of course, the smaller the diaphragm opening), the *greater* the depth of field.

LENSES FOR WILDLIFE PHOTOGRAPHY

There are nearly as many opinions on the best lenses for wildlife photography as there are photographers. And there are many telephoto options on the market. I can only pass along my personal preferences. In most situations Peggy and I depend on just two lenses for most big game shooting: one long and one short telephoto apiece, although we often carry others or at least have them handy.

Telephotos are lenses with longer than normal focal length (the distance from the front lens to the film). They magnify the size of the subject while transmitting it onto the film. If you have a telephoto lens on your camera, the deer will appear larger in your picture than if you are using the so-called normal 50mm lens that sees subjects as the naked eye would see them. Normal lenses are sold with most

Catadioptric lenses like this Vivitar Series 1 450mm employ mirrors to fold light. This allows a long focal length and high magnification with a lens that is physically short.

This highly rated Vivitar Series 1 70-210mm f/3.5 macro-focusing zoom lens is available in mounts for SLRs by most major makers. The cutaway photo shows the variety of screw and slide mounts needed for zoom focusing.

35 SLRs (although a 35 SLR camera body can be bought without a lens). If your telephoto lens is 100mm (or 2×), the image of the deer will be twice as large as with a 50mm lens. If it is 200 mm (or 4×), the image will be four times as large, and so forth.

Summed up, you do not have to approach as close to an animal with a telephoto as without one. In other words, a telephoto lens makes most of what we call "wildlife photography" possible.

Telephotos do have drawbacks, though. All except some extremely heavy ones are slower and are therefore more restricted to brighter-lit situations. Also, on telephotos, the depth of field is shallower, and this can be a disadvantage too. Subject movement—motion—is harder to arrest than with a short lens and thus you need to compensate by using a faster shutter speed.

It follows that telephoto lenses should be purchased with care. The natural inclination of enthusiastic novices is to buy the longest lens available. But the longer they are, the more difficult they are to hold steady while shooting. It is better for an inexperienced photographer to start with, say, a 200mm lens. Then, if all works well, he or she can graduate to something longer.

The long telephoto I prefer is a 400mm f/3.5, while Peggy carries a slightly shorter and lighter 300mm f/2.8. For closer work, both of us rely on the same 70–210mm zoom lenses. Since we carry the same brand of camera bodies, we can exchange lenses with each other. We also carry 1½× and 2× extenders that can be fitted between camera and telephoto lens to increase the focal length even farther. We only resort to the extenders when a nearer approach to the quarry is impossible or unadvisable. A 2× extender means the loss of two f/stops in the exposure, which you must remember to compensate for manually in your exposure settings.

This series of photographs made from the same camera position illustrates the enlargement values of various telephoto lenses as follow: 55mm Nikkor; 70–210 Vivitar zoom set at 70mm; 70–210 Vivitar zoom set at 210; 300mm Nikkor; 400mm Nikkor; 400mm Nikkor with 1.5 Vivitar teleconverter, equivalent to a 600mm lens. The same exposure was used on all.

55mm   43°   70mm   34°   210mm   12°

Between us, Peggy and I also carry a third short-focal-length lens: either a 55mm that also has macro (extreme closeup) capability, or a 35–85mm zoom (for wide-angle to short-telephoto zooming). We use the wider-angle settings for scenes, perhaps of deer habitat or winter range. We use the macro-setting for closeups of deer sign and tracks.

Here are the angles of coverage of lenses used to shoot the accompanying photographs.

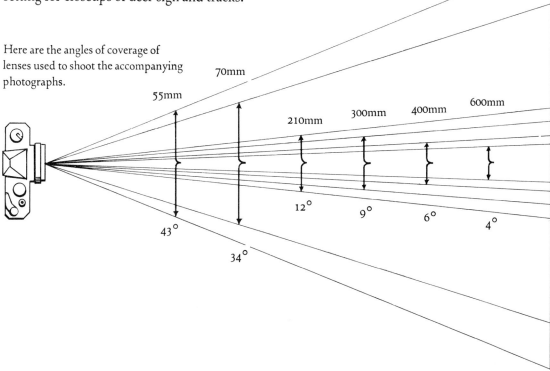

300mm 9°

400mm 6°

600mm 4°

Small tele-converters or extenders, which can be carried in a pocket, can increase the focal length of another lens by 50 or 100 percent. But you must compensate by increasing the exposure, which can be a handicap in poor light conditions or when shooting action.

LENS SHADES

Lens shades, also called lens hoods or sun-shades, are good investments. They protect lenses from direct rays of the sun when you are taking pictures. This protection, especially under a brilliant sun, improves the clarity and general quality of all photos. But lens shades are also easy to lose, so it is wise to keep them attached to a camera somehow. Many wildlife photographers connect the cap to the camera body or lens with a short length of mono-filament line. When shooting into the sun without a lens shade, substitute a hand, hat, or other handy object that casts a shadow over the front lens glass.

MOTOR DRIVE

We have equipped all of our 35mm SLRs with motor drives, which are both an advantage and a disadvantage. The disadvantage lies in the added weight, in the extra mechanism that might fail at a critical moment, and in their characteristic clinging noise that occasionally frightens wildlife. But all of these drawbacks are outweighed by two major benefits.

First, a motor drive makes following the action much easier—tracking a buck, for example. Second and more important, a motor drive lets you concentrate through the viewfinder. There is no need to deal with the distraction of manually advancing film. (The motor drive can also quickly rewind film. But this is only a minor advantage, because you can rewind almost as rapidly by hand while saving the drain on the batteries.)

The film strip here is called a black-and-white contact proof, which a photo lab makes by laying the negative strip almost directly against photosensitive paper. The lab can print a whole role of film in parallel strips on one 8x10-inch sheet called a proof or contact sheet. By studying the proofs on the contact with a magnifier, you can select the frames you want the lab to print as enlargements. I shot these five frames with a motor drive at about four frames per second. In frame 32A I had the buck in sharp focus, but I wasn't prepared for his breaking away in leaps and so wasn't able to keep him in sharp focus all the way, as you can see in the enlargements of frames 34A and 36A. When I can anticipate a deer's movement, a motor drive usually lets me get better results than this because it allows me to concentrate solely on composition and focus without also having to advance the film manually after each exposure.

Two f/numbers, or stops, overexposure—more than recommended by the camera's exposure meter

The accompanying frames illustrate the effects of overexposure and underexposure, as indicated. Remember, the smaller the f/number, the larger the aperture, and the greater the amount of light striking the film.

One f/number overexposure

Exactly on f/number recommended by camera's exposure meter

One f/number underexposure, allowing too little light to reach the film

Two f/numbers underexposure

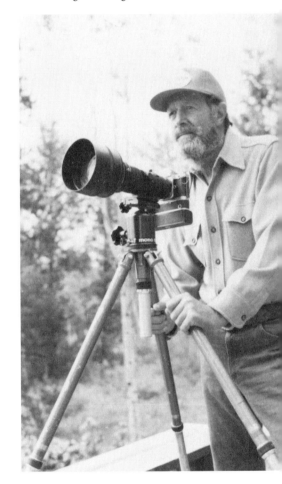

EXPOSURE

For automatic exposures, the exposure meter within the 35 SLR camera body is accurate enough for most deer photography. Nonetheless, I choose to set the camera on manual operation. Whenever possible, or whenever I am in doubt, I bracket exposures to be certain of the exposure. By "bracket," I mean shooting the same picture at either one stop or one-half stop above and below the exposure recommended by the meter. For more static photography, as from a blind or a fixed position, our spot exposure meter has been a very valuable addition to our gear. This gives an accurate reading on a very small area, say on the flank of a male deer standing in shade. But these meters are delicate and must be handled carefully. A good way to carry one is in a handmade holster (similar to a pistol holster) on the belt.

Still, an exposure meter is only an extra item to carry and possibly misplace or drop. As a substitute, it is certainly wise to carry along the exposure instructions that come with each roll of film. In a pinch, you can at least use these as a rough guide. Tape the instructions to some item of equipment or inside your equipment carrier so you don't lose them.

At the same time, keep the "16 method" exposure solution in mind. When photographing deer on perfectly clear days, with the sun at your back, the proper exposure setting will always include a shutter speed that closely matches the ISO (ASA) speed of your film. Here is how it works.

First set the lens opening at f/16. If the ISO (ASA) film speed is 25, set the shutter at 1/30 second, which is the closest setting to 25 you can make, and shoot. If using Kodachrome 64 (ISO/ASA 64) set the shutter at 1/75. If the ISO (ASA) is 100, set the shutter at 1/100, and so on.

There is one exception to the "16" rule: When shooting in bright sunlight over snow, where much light is reflected onto the subject, make one adjust-ment. In order to maintain some detail on the snow, and not have it appear entirely flat white, just change the base lens opening from f/16 to f/22 (closing the diaphragm one stop) and continue to set the shutter speed as above.

Over the years, I have learned that some exposure problems can be traced to built-in meters that are incorrectly calibrated. Such meters are set to slightly overexpose (which gives paler, more washed-out color than I like), perhaps because the manufacturers have concluded that most users are shooting color negative (print) film. That is fine if you want album snapshots rather than high-quality slides that can be projected on a screen or reproduced in magazines. Otherwise, I strongly suggest that you use color positive (slide) film. Color prints of all sizes can be made from the slides anyway, though at higher cost than prints from color print film.

To be certain about the accuracy of your camera meter, test it against the "16" method and also against the reading of a spot exposure meter or someone else's camera meter, which you know to be accurate. To achieve perfect exposures with your camera meter, you may have to change your ISO (ASA) dial to a different number as I have. When using Kodachrome 64, I now set the dial at 100.

FILM

A photographer has a wide choice of color and black-and-white films: slow and fast film, print (negative) or slide (positive) color film. Any film's speed refers to its sensitivity to light. Daylight (outdoors) films work best when there is much natural light, as in sunshine or during an otherwise bright day. Fast film responds more quickly to light and can be used when there is less of it, as on cloudy days or if you're deep in a deer woods.

Each roll of film has a film speed, or rating, expressed in numbers on each film box and canister. The faster the film, the higher the number. Until recently, film sold in America carried an ASA (American Standards Association) rating. Using the same numbers, film makers now use an ISO (International Standards Organization) rating, and may list film speed as ISO (ASA) 64 to assure you that ISO and ASA ratings are really the same.

Doubling the ISO (ASA) rating accounts for (or gains) one f/stop. ISO (ASA) 64 film is approximately twice as fast as 25. And ISO (ASA) 200 film is exactly twice as fast as 100, and so on.

Slower films are usually an outdoor photographer's best bet because they offer better contrast than fast film. Also, slower films are generally finer-grained, and therefore give sharper pictures. The drawback of slower films is their lower sensitivity to light; that is, they offer less flexibility when you are setting shutter speeds and f/stops. Slower films often require that you use larger diaphragm openings to gather enough light; this results in shallower depths of field, and also demands more precise focusing. Slower films may also require slower shutter speeds to gather enough light—speeds at which the camera must be held rock-steady to prevent blur. Faster films, on the other hand, are more forgiving of imprecision. But they tend to show coarser grain; also they give less contrast and lower resolution. For want of a better adjective, the color resulting from faster films often seems "flat" to me.

Peggy and I use Kodachrome 64 film almost exclusively because we prefer its usually rich color to the grayer or more bluish tones normally found in any of the faster films. Most of the photographs in this book were made with Kodachrome 64, which seems to me to give results that are as good as Kodachrome 25. Yet the 64 is twice as fast. Despite this, there is no denying that in certain dim light situations—such as deep in a forest—we have obtained more appealing deer photographs from faster Ektachrome 200 and 400 films. Again, the faster speeds certainly allow you more margin for error when shooting action pictures, as of running or fighting deer.

For a wildlife photographer scrambling about, a harness such as this is better than having a camera hang free from the neck or shoulder. This leaves hands free for climbing and other tasks, and keeps the camera handy.

When you stop to consider the time and money you may invest, it makes sense to shoot a lot of film. All films are outrageously expensive, but the cost may be negligible compared to the cost of your photographic trip. Far too often Peggy and I have regretted not shooting enough pictures of a particular deer, or of deer situations that we never saw again.

Once you've finished a photo session, don't leave the film in the camera for long just because a couple of exposures remain on the roll. This is false economy and a quick way to lose the entire roll. Have all film, especially color, developed immediately. Always avoid cut-rate or "drug store" photo finishing. All color film should be shipped promptly to a color lab of good reputation. Eastman Kodak film can be sent to any of the several Kodak labs located around the United States. But in my experience, even Kodak processing often leaves plenty to be desired. The quality control in recent years has been irregular. Check every Kodachrome slide for scratching, pits, and pockmarks that may have been inflicted during developing. The company is obligated to replace such damaged film and reimburse you for the cost of developing.

FILTERS

Although filters, available in many types and sizes, are useful in general photography, they have little if any application for photographing deer and most other wildlife. Normally a deer photographer seeks a perfectly natural outdoor image, exactly as his eye sees it. Most filters alter the natural color or effect. Also a filter is only another small item easily lost. And it is difficult to screw onto a lens when other exciting things are happening. Long ago, when I experimented with filters on wildlife, I found them to be unnecessary distractions.

STRAPS

The first thing to do after buying a new camera is to remove the narrow carrying strap that comes with it and throw it away. Also discard the camera's leather carrying case, which is next to useless. Replace the standard strap with a new wide one, say of two-inch webbing material. This is less likely to slide off the shoulder and will not cut into your shoulder or neck as a thin strap will.

When carrying the camera as you should, ready to use, around your neck, adjust the strap so that the camera rides high on your chest instead of bouncing on your stomach. For much rugged field use, consider buying a special camera harness as a replacement for the shoulder strap. A harness holds the camera, or even two cameras at once, onto your chest by means of straps crossed over the shoulder and around the back. The camera can be quickly released and then replaced in the harness, leaving both your hands free.

It is possible to sew a comfortable camera harness at home. Here's how the straps might look from the back. The camera can rest on the most comfortable place on the chest.

This fine telestock is adjustable in both length and shoulder-pod angle, allowing photographers of all sizes and shapes to use comfortably with various lenses and with or without motor drive. (Lepp Associates, Los Osos, CA.)

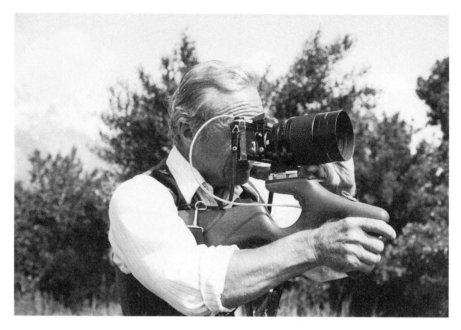

Many nature photographers prefer to mount their 35 SLRs on gunstocks. There are almost as many gunstock designs as ingenious photographers. Here, Frank Craighead, the biologist-photographer internationally known for his grizzly bear studies and National Geographic films, demonstrates use of a gunstock he designed and shaped to fit his own physique. Frank is using a Nikon camera and 500mm reflex lens. At rest, the gunstock is suspended from a shoulder sling.

SUPPORTS

Several fine professional cameramen I know use their 35 SLR cameras mounted on rifle stocks or similar shoulder-mounted devices for wildlife photography. They trip the shutter by pulling a trigger and achieve excellent results, especially with flying birds. I have never found a gunstock that helped me shoot as well as I can hand-holding or using a monopod or tripod. I advise using at least a monopod (or some similar firm rest) with any tele-photo lens at all. For most situations with lenses of 300mm or longer, I recommend using a sturdy tripod.

A lightweight tubular monopod, which collapses from about 60 inches extended down to 20 inches, can be conveniently carried in the hand or suspended from a backpack loop in the field. Good monopods are not expensive. In a pinch a monopod can serve as a walking stick or perhaps as a wading staff if you need to cross a creek while trailing a deer.

There is no substitute for a tripod when shooting from a blind or other fixed position. The main disadvantage of a heavier, bulkier tripod is that it restricts your maneuverability and is only truly

Peggy Bauer demonstrates how a three-section monopod fully extended can be used with a motor-driven camera and heavy 400mm telephoto lens. A monopod is much lighter and easier to carry than a tripod, although not as steady. It provides a much steadier camera base than hand-holding the camera and lens. And it can also be used as a wading or hiking staff.

This ultralight backpack tripod, which is roughly the same length as a monopod when collapsed, can be substituted for a monopod when you travel far on foot. Either unit fits neatly into a backpack and can be carried in the hand.

practical where the deer are not unduly wild or constantly moving. In the past I have missed many dramatic action pictures of big game, while still busy setting up or moving a tripod.

Few tripods or tripod heads are really adequate for most deer or wildlife photography. This is because they are generally designed with studio photographers in mind. To begin, most tripods that are light enough to carry easily are simply not sturdy enough, when fully extended, to hold a motor-driven camera with a heavy telephoto lens. Most of the heads presently available are even more inadequate. When using one, it is all but impossible to smoothly (without friction or binding) follow or track a moving creature. My solution has been to buy a too-heavy, but honestly sturdy, tripod that has legs which can be quickly and easily extended and adjusted to stand firmly on uneven terrain. Many tripods designed for studio work cannot be adjusted to stand up securely on a steep, rocky slope where deer may be. My tripod is a burden to

carry far and is at best a compromise, but it holds a heavy camera with long telephoto steady wherever I set it up.

Be especially selective when buying a tripod head, which is the vital link between your camera and its base. Almost without exception the ball-type heads, such as the expensive Swiss-made Monoball, are the best for all wildlife photography. A good head holds a camera exactly where you point it and does not allow the camera to suddenly fall over and crush your fingers. It allows you to shoot absolutely steady pictures even while you smoothly follow the action. Ideally, the following—panning—left or right, up or down, should be so smooth that you can concentrate totally on composition and focus.

This Monoball tripod head is about the best for wildlife photography.

This is the backpack and camera gear we used to shoot Carmen Mountains whitetails along the Rio Grande River in west Texas. We usually pack a large canteen of water and high-caloric snacks.

Also I prefer a quick-release camera mount to a screw-on mount on my tripod head. If you install small adapter plates on your cameras and on longer telephoto lenses, the quick-release feature permits mounting or changing the camera on the tripod in only a second or two. Once in place, the camera remains *secure*, unable to turn or work loose on a stud screw. The best ball-type tripod heads are quite expensive, but they are worth the money in smooth operation and photo results.

More than one photographer we know has encountered trouble when he couldn't find the stud screw from his tripod, a critical piece that is easily lost. Why not carry an extra?

You don't need an expensive array of equipment, such as this, for top-quality deer photos. But if you have two camera bodies, you can increase the salability of your photos by simultaneously shooting both color and black-and-white film with lenses of differing powers.

FAMILIARITY WITH YOUR EQUIPMENT

No matter what the brand of camera or lenses, become thoroughly familiar with everything. Study the camera manual carefully, and then practice shooting the camera with various lenses around home and anywhere you go. Take pictures of the kids, the neighbors, the family pets, even passing cars. The object is to increase your familiarity with the equipment. Zoos and local game parks are fine places to go for practice.

Shoot empty at first. After you've done that for a while, load the camera with black-and-white film, which is cheaper than color, to test yourself. Always concentrate on rapid handling and on fast but sharp focus. Sharpness should be the first consideration; speed will come with practice. Drills that may seem useless at first will eventually pay off in deer pictures that you can brag about. Most encounters with deer are fleeting, and you must make the most of your few opportunities.

PHYSICAL CONDITIONING

You may think it odd of me to speak of the need for getting into good physical condition for wildlife photography. But being in shape can be important when hunting deer with a camera. Here's an illustration.

One photo outfit I use on somewhat wary deer weighs close to 30 pounds altogether. It consists of my tripod and ball-head, my 35 SLR with motor drive, plus the jumbo 400mm f/3.5 telephoto lens. I must carry all of this on my shoulder, assembled and ready to use. This limits my mobility and tends to discourage long hikes in rough country. So, to some extent, I try to pick my photography sites very carefully. But that isn't always possible or sensible, so strong legs and lungs come in handy.

One November morning I lugged the gear up to a knoll that overlooked a small alpine basin where I had found much deer activity the day before. The climb up the mountainside was terrible. I was carrying the 30-pound camera outfit plus other gear. Halfway there, with lungs on fire and heart pounding, I wondered about my sanity. But I made the ascent and was completely set up and ready to shoot when the sunrise revealed two handsome mule deer bucks in the basin. The wilderness scene was astonishingly beautiful—one I would never have been able to photograph if I had been out of condition.

There are a good many ways to achieve better physical condition, and some of them are pleasant. Daily hiking and jogging are among the easiest. Walk rather than ride to work if that is at all feasible. Climb staircases rather than use elevators. Bicycling is great. In winter cross-country skiing is a splendid conditioner. Doing such household chores as lawn mowing at double speed is not only a good way to shape up, but it also creates more time for getting out in the woods.

Pursuing any wildlife with a camera, motor drive and a heavy telephoto lens requires strong arms. Again, all that gear is heavy to carry. Also, a photographer is often required to hold all of it motionless and ready to shoot for long periods, muscles flexed and tense, while waiting for a deer to move into a better position. That explains why some very good wildlife photographers I know participate in a year-round program of arm and shoulder exercise. Weight lifting and pushups are good arm conditioners.

FOOTGEAR

Peggy and I depend heavily on some other equipment when stalking deer, and several of these items are nearly as important as the cameras and optics. Footwear, for example, is critical. With rare exceptions I have never been able to take top-quality pictures of deer without walking (often for long distances), wading streams, or climbing on rough trails. A wildlife photographer should consequently have a pair of comfortable, sturdy, ankle-high boots

The difference between poor and excellent wildlife pictures might well be in the footgear you wear. Boots that are comfortable, well broken in, and even waterproof will help you reach, and survive in, deer country.

with lug-type soles. They should be completely broken in, and it helps if they have been waterproofed. In rattlesnake country, you might want to wear higher boots. In winter, insulated footgear helps. I have used gaiters to good advantage when filming in deep snow.

PACKS

A backpack or a belt pack can be valuable. (Most manufactured camera bags, which must be slung over one shoulder, are impractical in the wild.) The backpack holds much more gear than the belt pack, which straps securely around the waist. But the belt pack is handier in some situations.

For a long time my favorite backpack has been a lightweight exterior frame model. The bag is multi-compartmented. The separate storage pockets keep certain items in a particular place, always available for immediate use. Unexposed film, for example, goes in one side pocket, but is placed in the opposite side after it has been exposed. In addition to all the necessary photo gear, the backpack also holds a jacket, a poncho or an ultralight "bicyclist" rainsuit, high-energy snacks, insect repellent, a canteen of water, a cap, and gloves. All of this means extra weight, of course, but it also enables us to stay in the field for a long time if necessary. For locating mule deer far from a base camp or trailhead, we have often camped right on the spot by carrying a light tent and sleeping bags.

Peggy uses a Coleman Peak 1 backpack frame and bag to carry camera equipment on a Wyoming trail. The frame rides comfortably on the hips, and the bag's many compartments and pockets keep items separate and handy.

Pocket and compartment details are shown here for the 765 Peak 1 pack, which we have used to carry both our cameras and overnight camping gear. The 705 Peak 1 day sack is suitable for day-trip filming situations.

Many excellent day packs and belt packs, such as these by Camp Trails, are available for toting a good bit of camera equipment in the field. Packs leave the hands free for shooting. Such carriers should be made of waterproof material.

Belt packs, or fanny packs, give you easy access to small amounts of gear.

Saddlebags that are specially built with compartments or dividers make for safer transport of photographic equipment. Cameras may be reached from either the saddle or from the ground.

This case by Pelican is waterproof, dustproof, and extremely tough, yet it is fairly lightweight. It offers excellent gear protection for travel by air and car—and for storage, as well. The case can be carried aboard an airplane, and it fits under the seat.

A lightweight backpack tent is a boon for backcountry wildlife photography. Often we have found mule deer too far away for easy daily access. But with a tent, we can camp in deer country. This expedition model by R.E.I. of Seattle is roomy and can withstand high winds and the foulest weather. We have pitched it in all conditions from Texas to Alaska.

Peggy and I happen to be filming a pair of cow elk in this picture. We've found that cross-country skis are the best means for reaching mule deer in midwinter when snows are deep.

GOING IN SNOW

Peggy and I often use snowshoes and cross-country skis for winter photography, especially when deer are concentrated in a few limited areas. The skis are usually better than the webs for speed and distance. We substitute our ski poles, as monopod or bipod, for a tripod.

Peggy Bauer demonstrates how to use ski or snowshoe poles as a bipod when photographing wildlife. Winter is an ideal time for finding mule deer.

CARE OF EQUIPMENT

A wildlife photographer is likely to give all of his equipment rougher than normal treatment. Consequently, he must provide special care and maintenance. Always keep all lenses clean. Optical glass is softer than other kinds of glass, and the coating used on a lens is extremely thin. Dry dust should be removed with a soft camel's-hair brush, or you should blow it off with a small ear syringe. Never blow (by mouth) or breathe on a lens element. Your breath contains moisture that will leave a film on the glass and affect its ability to transmit light.

Never touch lens surfaces with your fingers. Fingerprints contain acid perspiration that can actually etch the glass and damage it permanently. If you accidentally touch the surface with your fingers, polish the glass gently with a special lens-cleaning tissue. Do not use the tissue dry. Instead, add a drop or two of a good commercial lens cleaner and apply gently with a circular motion.

Avoid using a handkerchief or other cloth to wipe a lens because the lens can be scratched by dust or grit embedded in the fabric. Facial tissues aren't very good either, because they leave residues of dust and lint on the lens. Some tissues actually abrade glass.

Absolutely never tinker with the mechanical elements of a lens. It is strictly a job for specialists. You are asking for trouble if you attempt to grease or otherwise lubricate the moving parts of your camera. Lubricants thicken in cold weather, and that means the camera may not operate when you need it most—when deer are most active. To spare ourselves mechanical problems, Peggy and I always carry at least one extra camera body that either one of us can use as a substitute in a pinch. More than once, the spare body has saved a photo hunt, because even the best camera gear can suddenly break down.

To keep my cameras and lenses clean, I carry along a soft camel-hair brush, a plastic container of lens cleaner, and soft lens tissues. Some photographers also carry cans of compressed air to blow dust and grit from equipment.

Take advantage of any available solid object such as a rock or tree for an even *firmer* position than offered free-hand.

Lacking a tripod for a 400mm tele-photo lens, rest the lens on a rock or other firm base, using gloves, a cap, a sweater, or other clothing as a pad. Otherwise, camera shake will blur the photo.

DEER SHOOTING STRATEGY

Deer photography demands two different strategies, depending on whether you're in open-hunting areas or in wildlife sanctuaries. To film in areas open to hunting requires being as inconspicuous as humanly possible all of the time. In other words, there's need for woodsmanship. It means using stealth plus all the camouflage and stalking skills a gun hunter needs, and then some. The object is to see deer, the closer the better, long before the deer spots you. All of this is very demanding, but if you can shoot a good picture of a nice buck this way, you have something worth bragging about. In fact, that photo will represent a far greater achievement than would the stuffed head of the same deer.

Photographing in a sanctuary area requires an entirely different technique. Strange as it may seem, I always try to stay within the deer's sight rather than try to stay concealed. That way, the wary animal may feel relatively unthreatened as long as it can keep an eye on me. Of course, many sanctuary deer will run from me, or at least keep a great distance between us so my strategy fails in those cases. But enough deer remained unalarmed to make my

Peggy Bauer demonstrates the proper
way to hold a 35mm SLR with a short
telephoto lens and motor drive. Weight
of the unit is supported by both hands.
While the left hand focuses, the right
forefinger is on shutter release. Holding the camera this way, you can track
a moving target comfortably.

At times it is possible to photograph
from a vehicle window using either a
clampod on the door or a pad to cush-
ion and steady the camera. In most
places, deer will let you approach
closer in a vehicle than on foot.

method worthwhile. By staying in full view, I have
been able to approach to within telephoto range of
some splendid deer.

It is a mistake to directly advance on any deer
or other animal that is accustomed to people, even
in a national park. Too often they will simply drift
away. Patience becomes a great virtue for a deer
photographer. It is far wiser to proceed on an angle,
pausing often, moving slowly and without sudden
movements, while never staring or concentrating
too much on your intended target.

Peggy takes advantage of quaking aspen tree trunks for a steady photographic position. She is also fairly well concealed from several sides, and camouflage clothing helps her blend in. Mule deer often pass very close to this vantage.

Conifers can be used to conceal much of you, while minimizing contrast behind your shoulders and head.

This one-man photo blind by George Lepp measures 4x4x5 feet and is supported by plastic pipe that is color coded for easy assembly. Camo-cloth windows allow you to see out without being seen. (Photo by Lepp Associates, Los Osos, CA.)

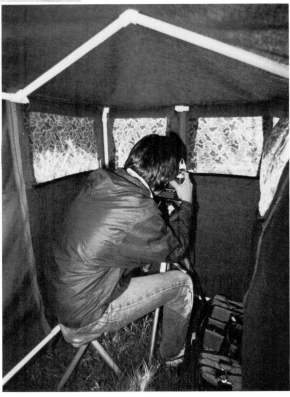

When a larger, frame blind is impractical, you may need only disguise your own outline to allay the fears of an animal. This "hat blind" by George Lepp allows you to see the subject through camo-cloth mesh before peering through the camera viewfinder. (Photo by Lepp Associates.)

In a pinch, a hastily constructed blind of old canvas cloth such as this may serve for deer photography along a busy trail. But this does not offer the best possible concealment. The rips in the cloth were made by a black bear.

This splendid, easy-to-pitch portable canvas blind is light in weight and excellent for all kinds of wildlife photography. Zippered windows at different levels and on all sides make shooting convenient. The tent blind is manufactured by Eureka! Tents in Binghamton, New York.

Avoid direct, prolonged eye contact. Many deer do not like to be watched intently. By being patient, by taking plenty of time, it is often possible to walk much nearer while seldom looking at the deer at all. When in the vicinity of deer, I often sit down for a while and look in another direction, especially if there are clouds overhead. I allow the clouds to pass and the sun to fall on the scene. I'm convinced that deer will frequently remain nearby just to be able to keep an eye on me.

One person can approach deer more easily, more closely, than two, and two more easily than three, and so forth. Many creatures tend to be **in**timidated in direct ratio to how greatly they are outnumbered. Deer will almost certainly react and flush if two photographers try to advance from opposite sides at once. Also avoid blocking a deer's

The usefulness of a photo blind depends on its placement, and on your ingenuity. This was originally designed as a cornfield, goose-shooting blind, but is just as effective as a photo blind. The photographer can simply stand up and walk away with it if he wants to shoot from a better position.

line of retreat, such as by moving between a deer, which is standing in an open meadow, and the nearest heavy cover.

In most wildlife sanctuaries where there is no hunting, bucks seem no more or less wary than does. However, during the rut, they may be a little less wary, which makes autumn a worthwhile and very active time to concentrate on photography. In many regions fall foliage at that time provides colorful backgrounds.

EXPLOITING THE WEATHER—AND COPING

Every outdoor photographer is eventually doomed to wait out what seems to be interminable bad weather. But bad weather may be the prelude to some outstanding photographic opportunities.

The passing of a storm front, the scudding of squalls on the horizon, and the clearing of angry skies all offer unique opportunities (as well as dramatic light) for shooting scenes of ominous beauty. Try to find deer and fit them into the scenes. Watch for the roving spotlights of sun that may penetrate a black sky and illuminate certain parts of the landscape. Be ready when the spotlight falls on your subject. Also remember to keep your equipment entirely dry.

A little moisture seeping into the moving parts of cameras or into lenses can cause terrible problems. When in the rain, we work under tough, waterproof ponchos that will not puncture when we must hurry through brittle brush. We always carry enough plastic bags to protect all of our equipment in wet weather. Once back in a sheltered place, we immediately wipe our equipment dry with absorbent cloth.

To some extent it is possible to predict your local weather and thereby make better use of your time. A few facts are worth noting. High clouds are unlikely to rain on you no matter how ominous they may appear. On the other hand, beware of low and lowering dark cloud banks. Odors are stronger before rain, so much so that you can often smell rain approaching. Expect precipitation when distant sounds are low and hollow, because low clouds act as sounding boards. Leaves begin to show their undersides and deer tend to be more nervous, more active, when a storm is in the offing.

Cold weather, particularly intensely cold weather, presents its own set of problems to camera and camera toter. You either dress properly or stay indoors. We prefer to use the layering system of dressing to go outdoors. That means we wear several layers of light garments rather than one very warm piece of clothing. This allows us to add or remove layers as the temperature changes, or as our physical activities increase or decrease. If we travel vigorously on skis, for example, we need fewer layers to keep warm. But to stand still in one place, we must add layers. The unworn clothing goes into the backpack, where it remains handy. We always try to remove unneeded layers *before* we begin to perspire.

Starting from the inside, the first piece is polypropylene underwear long enough so that it doesn't creep up your arms and legs as you exert

Trees can provide deer hunter with both concealment and a good all-around view. A lightweight rope ladder can make access to a tree crown or tree blind relatively easy.

Even under the best conditions, cameras used extensively outdoors can get dirty and wet. So it makes sense to carry camera gear in puncture-proof plastic containers when not actually in use. We make considerable use of clear, zip-lock bags.

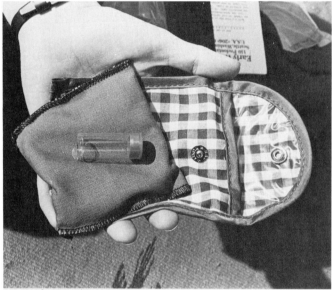

A handwarmer like this, fueled with water and carbide crystals, is helpful during cold-weather photography. I carry one or two in a jacket pocket on the bitterest days. The warmers are available by mail from Early Winters in Seattle.

yourself. Next come woolen pants and shirt, not too tight, with the shirt having an extra-long tail. A sweater and finally a jacket or parka make up the two outer layers. I wear two pairs of woolen socks inside leather boots, usually with felt innersoles. Snowmobile boots are excellent if the photography is sedentary. I always wear a warm hat that covers my whole head, including the back of my neck, because much body heat can escape there. Prescription sunglasses are essential when traveling over bright snow.

Hands are the hardest of all to keep warm. We solve the problem with down mittens attached to a cord through the sleeves of our jackets. In this way we cannot inadvertently drop or misplace the mittens when handling the camera. But mittens alone may not be enough. I also carry chemical handwarmers in my pockets when I'm out on severely cold days. Another tip is to wear light shooting gloves with fingertips missing inside the down mittens, which can be removed for a few minutes at a time.

It is just as necessary to keep your camera and film fairly warm during very cold temperatures. I

Winter creates extra problems for wildlife photographers. One of the most difficult tasks is keeping the hands warm when handling cold metal equipment. We often wear wool-knit shooting gloves without fingertips inside heavier down mittens. To prevent losing the mittens, we attach them to our jacket sleeves. That way we can slip our hands in and out of the mittens easily without fear of leaving them behind. In extremely cold weather, we also carry carbide hand warmers (right) in our jacket pockets.

carry both inside my outermost jacket or layer to take advantage of heat trapped there. Film becomes brittle and can crack if advanced carelessly in deep cold. Too-cold batteries will not provide enough power for motor drives, and cold exposure meters give inaccurate readings. Avoid bringing very cold camera equipment suddenly into a warm place, where metal and glass parts will become badly fogged.

We have also spent much time photographing deer in hot, dry places. Here it is always necessary to keep film out of the sun and in the coolest spots possible. Never, absolutely never, leave film on the dashboard of a car where it will bake and be ruined. Also avoid leaving a camera lying out unshaded in the sun. In the field, we often protect film in a cooler. At home, we store it in the refrigerator.

Dust and blowing sand can be as destructive as moisture if they get inside cameras and lenses. A single grain of grit can scratch roll after roll of film without your knowledge. Not until after the film is developed is the terrible scratch apparent. We use the same plastic bags to protect all of our gear when shooting in arid areas, or whenever the wind blows excessively, as we do in wet conditions.

SEASONS

Timing is very important in deer photography. I have already emphasized the importance of filming early and late in the day. But seasons must also be considered. Late spring through early summer is the period when fawns still have white camouflage spots and when photos of fawns against fresh green vegetation are most appealing. Midsummer finds all native deer in their red-colored coats, the males still with antlers in velvet. Late autumn is the time to search for trophy bucks, with necks swollen, majestic and hyperactive during the peak of the rut.

A cap with a long bill is ideal when using a 35 SLR in bright sunlight. It reduces reflections and keeps the sun out of your eyes.

Perhaps the most exciting time, the period of the most action, is in early fall. That's when we look for young or medium-size bucks. Like young males anywhere, human and otherwise, these young deer are not yet "established" in the world. They are constantly looking for trouble, competing and jostling with one another. They are also very restless and therefore much easier to find. If you can find an area frequented by junior bucks, and they do tend to gather in small bands, you should also have plenty of activity to photograph.

STOPPING THE ACTION

The more and faster the action, the harder it is to concentrate on sharp focus and on composition. But it is essential to remember these points. Far too many pictures of wild action turn out to be useless because the animals are blurred or so out of focus as to be almost indistinguishable.

When aiming at action, immediately set a fast shutter speed, or rather the fastest shutter speed that the existing light (and your light meter) will allow. I like to use 1/1000 second whenever possible, and it *is* possible in bright light with 64 speed film (as at f/3.5). I usually prefer a picture that is slightly underexposed. An exposure of 1/500 will also "stop" most deer action, while 1/250 second is borderline. These slower speeds will not freeze a deer in full flight. Keep in mind that an animal crossing in front of you requires a faster shutter speed than one approaching you or going away.

Shots of running deer that are in focus with the action "stopped" are the most difficult of all to get. Such action shots require that you shoot plenty of film to get only one or two photos just right. Fast handling is necessary, and that comes only from practice and familiarity with the camera.

Rattling sometimes pays off. This whitetail buck came to the rattling from an unexpected direction and was "shot" just as it turned to run away.

This splendid whitetail buck is another that could not resist investigating the sound of our rattled antlers. It approached to within 50 feet of our blind. Unfortunately, vegetation blocked too much of the lens—and the sound of my trying to raise the camera a little higher spooked him.

This is not a trophy whitetail buck, but it does have an attractive face—all of which is in crisp focus.

SHARP PICTURES

After setting a fast shutter speed, the next consideration must be focus. Sometimes there is opportunity for extremely careful, sharp focus. On other occasions things happen too quickly. Anyone viewing a wildlife photo is first drawn to the animal's eyes, so whenever possible I focus on that bright eye, on the wet muzzle, or—in the case of large bucks—on the burl at the base of the antler. There is enough detail in all of these areas to achieve perfect focus, and if the deer's eye is genuinely sharp, the whole picture will almost surely be in focus. At the least the focus will make the shot attractive.

When looking through your viewfinder, watch especially for a catchlight in the deer's eyes. This white reflected highlight from the sun or sky makes the deer look alive and distinguishes a dynamic from an ordinary shot.

By focusing on the eye of this mule deer buck, we also have the ears and base of the antlers in good detail. The large ears and black forehead distinguish the mule deer from the whitetail.

The difference between a good and a poor wildlife photograph is often in relative sharpness of focus. When filming deer, focus on the eye or the wet shiny nose.

I normally prefer a fast shutter speed to compensate for unsteadiness when I'm hand-holding a camera. But for this shot, I sat down, rested the camera on a knee, and shot at 1/30 second to "catch" the snowflakes. The flakes would have been barely visible at, say, 1/250 second.

It pays to keep a camera handy and always set at the proper exposure. That way you can sometimes get shots of a deer's first recognition of you, a moment when the deer is suddenly alert. When a whitetail's tail is up, with rump patch flared in alarm, shoot quickly and be ready to shoot again because the deer will probably soon take off.

If you are not satisfied with the sharpness of your pictures, the problem might not be your failure to focus correctly. The trouble may be with camera movement or optics. I never shoot a deer picture hand-holding the camera while standing up if I am able to either sit down or steady the camera against some stationary object. When sitting down it is possible to use the knees and body as the three legs of a tripod. Some of the accompanying photographs illustrate the proper way to hold a camera and how to take advantage of a firm camera rest. I also don't like to hand-hold a camera at speeds slower than 1/250 second, although I will do so if I have no other choice. A monopod or tripod can also eliminate most camera movement. Some kind of soft pad or clampod will let you take steady photographs through the window of your vehicle.

If the problem of blurred or soft-focus photos is optical, it may be that you have the wrong focusing screen (for you) inside your viewfinder, or one that is not compatible with your eyesight. Most 35 SLR camera systems offer a variety of screens, and the one for general photography (sold with the camera box) is not always the best for telephoto photography. Others are available, and most are inexpensive. Eyeglasses with bifocals can make focusing difficult. But a good optometrist may be able to prescribe glasses that work well for you— or even prescribe glass for your camera viewfinder.

COMPOSITION

Composition may be the most difficult aspect of wildlife photography to discuss because beauty—which in this case constitutes a good deer picture—is entirely in the eye of the beholder. Good composition is easier to sense than describe. But I will make a few suggestions here anyway.

For the most striking, dramatic photos, try to keep the deer away from dead center of the picture. Instead, have the animal appear to be entering the photograph by leaving a little more space in *front* of it than behind. You must do this consciously through the viewfinder, because the natural tendency is to center right on the subject as if aiming with the crosshairs of a riflescope.

Of course, few wild deer give you much time to ponder perfect composition. If the animal is fairly calm and not too anxious to run away, however, study the entire composition in your viewfinder a little more carefully. Shoot one exposure and then check yourself. If there is any distracting object in the scene, move or shift your viewpoint just enough to remove it. For example, a tree or bush that seems to be growing out of a deer's head can ruin the whole composition. You might be able to remove that distraction by moving yourself one step left or right.

If you are lucky or skilled enough to be very close to a deer, be careful that you do not cut off antler tips, legs, or other body parts. A lot of otherwise fine animal pictures are ruined that way. Unless you are shooting especially for a head shot, make an effort to get the whole deer in the picture.

It is vital to avoid having a horizon line, or any distinct dividing line, cut across the middle of the frame. Like having the subject at dead center, this can also render a picture too static. If your deer is

Every photographer can count on a few surprises. While I was focusing on the doe from my ground level blind, another deer head suddenly popped up in the background. But the second had antlers! It vanished in the next instant.

PHOTO MISTAKES

During a career spent hunting deer with a camera, I have made all the mistakes it is possible to make. When photographing such an elusive creature as the whitetail, flawed pictures are far more the rule than the exception.

This could have been a much better buck photo. First, the focus is not sharp enough, especially considering that the subject is motionless. I should also have waited for a better pattern of sunlight to shift onto the face and antlers. Most of the time a photographer had better shoot while he can and hope for a better chance soon after. Mine never came; a moment later this deer was gone.

A hand-held, long focal length lens, plus grainy film was responsible for this imperfect study of a whitetail buck. But for a deer with trophy antlers such as this, any close-up at all is not a bad one.

I should have spent more time with this California mule deer, first by trying to maneuver into a better position for better composition, and second by striving for sharper focus. Here also the foreground is much too distracting.

Timing is important, too, in deer photography. This frame was snapped a split second too late, or perhaps too early. As a result there is no clear view of the deer.

Here an otherwise excellent action photo of two whitetail does in a dispute was ruined when I cut off the head of one. These mistakes can sometimes be avoided by anticipating such action and adjusting the camera angle accordingly. In the viewfinder, leave room all around for action to take place.

These could have been great shots of
running animals, but I was caught by
surprise. My shutter speed was not set
fast enough to really freeze the deer
in midstride.

willing, try moving around it and shooting from various angles, including directly into the sun. I have a strong preference for side-lit wildlife subjects. For an unusual angle of a deer, try dropping flat to the ground and shooting up to get a gopher's viewpoint. But I admit that I have frightened away some otherwise calm deer by doing this. Maybe they thought I had turned into a coyote.

Better picture composition can be achieved through contrast, which is nothing more than the difference in brightness. The greatest contrast is obtained by placing very dark subjects against very light backgrounds, or vice versa. The least contrast occurs when the subject and the background are of equal light values. Big game and deer pictures with greatest impact are often those which show the animal in greatest contrast to its environment. Such a shot might have the sunlight illuminating the face and antlers of a buck standing in an otherwise dark forest. Or it might have a dark deer outlined against a snowbank, or a reddish, spotted fawn in the fresh green vegetation of early summer.

Always watch for any impending action—for a deer ready to dart away, for example—and allow room in the viewfinder (in *front* of the deer) for the action to take place.

This is a wild buck in an open hunting area of Ohio. I made a successful stalk on the animal and could easily have shot it with a rifle and maybe with a bow and arrow. But this southern exposure of a northbound buck is my only "trophy" with a hand-held camera. There simply was no time for accurate focus. I just aimed and shot.

LEARNING BY DOING

Although it is good to read about photography, and worthwhile to talk shop with other wildlife photographers, the best lessons come from actually taking photographs and then analyzing the results. Devote plenty of time to studying the pictures you have made. Project the slides onto the screen to see where you have made mistakes, and to consider what you might have done better. If too many pictures are fuzzy, try to determine why—and correct the problem the next time out. A slide enlarged hundreds of times on a screen can reveal many shortcomings not evident when holding the slide up to your eye.

Most texts on wildlife photography, this chapter included, probably concentrate too much advice on what to do and what not to do in too little space. Most of this is derived from the writer's personal experiences and peculiar circumstances. I happen to live in good deer country and have ample opportunities to observe deer. But you are well advised to follow your own instincts, while gaining experience and using this book as only a rough guide. This book should help you start out right and avoid some pitfalls. Yet lessons learned from trial and error are usually very well learned. Any deer photographer is bound to make many mistakes and have many disappointments, but he may also end up with a portfolio of outstanding deer photographs. We hope so, anyway.

There is one way in which we *can* be of great help, and that is on where to go. There is a surprising number of good camera hunting places for deer and other wildlife across North America. These are mostly our national parks, our national wildlife refuges, some state and county parks, plus a scattering of private refuges open to the public. All of these in the western United States are listed and described in my state-by-state guide, *Photographing the West*.

A diffused low-afternoon sun provided just the right eye highlighting for this muley portrait.

INDEX